THE INVESTOR'S MIND

The Pause Framework for Better Decisions

SAJAL KAPOOR

notionpress.com

INDIA • SINGAPORE • MALAYSIA

ISBN
Paperback 979-8-90479-796-6
Hardcase 979-8-90479-798-0

Contents

MOVEMENT III – The Bridge

MOVEMENT IV – Heuristics for Better Judgement

Closing

INTRODUCTION

HOW TO READ THIS BOOK

We like to believe better decisions come from more information. In practice, they come from better thinking.

The problem is not what we know.

It is how quickly we act on what we think we know.

Our minds move fast. We simplify before we understand. We trust patterns, stories, and instincts long before we examine them. Most of this happens quietly, which is why it is so easy to miss.

This book is about making that hidden process visible and usable.

THE PAUSE

Every decision passes through a moment you rarely notice.

Something happens.

You react.

In between, there is a pause.

Most of the time, it disappears.

But that small gap—between what happens and what you do next—shapes outcomes more than the information you have.

This book is about learning to see that pause—and use it.

At its core is a simple loop:

Pause → Examine → Decide → Review

You will see this pattern repeatedly—across mistakes, biases, and decisions—before we bring it together at the end.

A LESSON FROM CRICKET

In cricket, the difference between control and error often comes down to timing.

What makes certain bowlers difficult is not just skill, but their ability to disrupt that timing.

Jasprit Bumrah does this through his action and disguise. His short run-up and slight hesitation before release delay the moment the ball leaves his hand. The batsman expects one rhythm—but receives another. That fraction of a second is enough to break instinct and force uncertainty.

Ravichandran Ashwin achieved a similar effect differently. At times, he varies his delivery stride with subtle pauses. The batsman, already committed to a movement, is forced to adjust mid-action. The hesitation creates doubt—and doubt creates mistakes.

And then there is the late Shane Warne.

Warne's pause was not mechanical. It was psychological.

Before the ball was even delivered, he created a moment through presence, eye contact, or a brief delay. The batsman was already thinking, already reacting. The contest often began before the ball left his hand.

Across all three, the principle is the same:

They interrupt automatic responses.

They create hesitation.

They force awareness where there was none.

Good thinking works in exactly the same way.

Most mistakes do not come from a lack of intelligence. They come from acting without noticing.

The *pause* is what interrupts that.

WHAT THIS BOOK DOES

This is not a book of answers. It does not eliminate uncertainty.

Instead, it offers something more practical:

A way to think more clearly in a world that will never be fully certain.

It will not make you right.

It will help you be less wrong—more consistently.

The ideas here draw from thinkers such as Daniel Kahneman, Charlie Munger, Nassim Nicholas Taleb, and others who have studied how decisions actually work.

They are not original in isolation.

What is different is how they are structured and how they are used together.

This book builds a simple system around a practical observation:

Better decisions do not come from more thinking.

They come from better moments of thinking.

And those moments begin with a pause.

WHY THE CHAPTERS ARE SHORT

The chapters are intentionally short.

Each one is designed to stand on its own:

one idea

one case

one lesson

one set of limits (for heuristics)

In a world of fractured attention, this matters.

The repetition is deliberate. Each idea appears in different contexts, so you can recognise it when it matters. The same concept often reveals something new when applied to a different situation.

This is not a book to be read once.

It is meant to be used.

WHAT THIS BOOK IS

This is a book about how thinking fails and how to improve it.

You will learn to:

See where judgement breaks down.

Recognise patterns that mislead you.

Use simple tools to make better decisions under uncertainty.

These tools are called heuristics.

They do not eliminate errors.

They help reduce them.

WHAT THIS BOOK IS NOT

This is not investment advice.

It is not a recommendation to buy or sell any stock, nor a guide to constructing a portfolio.

The ideas here are meant to improve how you think—not to replace your judgement.

You must make your own decisions.

HOW THE BOOK WORKS

The book moves through four layers:

1. **How thinking works**

   Understanding the mind—fast, automatic, and often misleading

2. **Where thinking breaks**

   Biases that distort judgement in predictable ways

3. **Why heuristics exist**

   The gap between knowing and doing

4. **How to think better**

   Practical tools that work under real conditions

Each chapter follows a simple structure:

- The idea
- How it applies
- Where it fails

Because every tool works and every tool has limits.

HOW TO USE THIS BOOK

You do not need to read it in order.

You can start anywhere:

With a bias that feels familiar,

with a heuristic you want to use,

or with a situation you are trying to understand.

This is a toolbox, not a sequence.

The most important moments in this book are when something feels:

obvious,

urgent,

certain.

Those are the moments when thinking is weakest.

And when a pause matters most.

BEFORE YOU BEGIN

You already have a way of thinking.

This book will not replace it.

It will make you aware of it and give you a way to adjust it.

Some ideas will feel simple. Others may take time to settle.

That is expected.

You are not learning how to be right every time.

You are learning how to be less wrong and to recognise when it matters most.

Because, in the end, the quality of your decisions depends less on what happens and more on what you do in the pause before you act.

MOVEMENT I – HOW THINKING WORKS

The Illusion of Rational Thinking

You don't repeat mistakes—you repeat patterns you haven't seen yet.

THE CASE

As a child, I had a habit of opening every new toy within hours of receiving it. Not to break it, but to understand how it worked. Taking things apart felt like solving a puzzle in reverse. It was absorbing and satisfying in the moment.

There was always a consequence. Once opened, the toy rarely worked the same way again.

At the time, it did not feel like a mistake. It felt like learning.

What was missing was a simple question about what would happen next.

Years later, the same pattern showed up in investing. This was around 1994.

With limited money, each decision felt urgent. Opportunities like IPOs carried excitement, strong narratives and the fear of missing out. It felt like acting quickly mattered more than being right. That made it easy to say yes without slowing down.

Most decisions came from instinct rather than analysis. The thinking came afterwards, usually in the form of justification.

The result was predictable. Almost all of the capital was lost.

Recovery came through circumstance rather than skill. Finishing engineering and finding a job via campus placement made it possible to rebuild. But the deeper lesson was not clear at the time.

Only later did the connection become obvious.

Opening toys without thinking ahead and rushing into investments came from the same pattern. In both cases, curiosity and instinct led, while reflection came too late.

The action came first. The thinking came later—usually as justification.

THE REALISATION

That pattern did not come from investing. It was already there.

Investing simply exposed it.

What felt like independent decisions were often variations of the same underlying behaviour. The environment changed, but the pattern stayed the same.

This is where self-awareness starts to matter.

It is not about removing instinct or curiosity. It is about noticing the moment before you act. That small gap is where control exists.

Without that *pause*, patterns repeat automatically. With it, they can be seen and changed.

THE PRINCIPLE

Self-awareness is the ability to notice your own mind as it works. It means stepping back and observing your thoughts instead of being carried along by them.

Most behaviour follows patterns shaped by earlier experience. These patterns guide actions in the same way a train follows its tracks. Real self-awareness begins when you see that you are not the script, but the one watching it.

In *Thinking, Fast and Slow,* Daniel Kahneman describes two systems of thought. System 1 is fast, automatic, and intuitive. System 2 is slower and more deliberate. Most mistakes happen when the fast system acts unchecked, and the slower system only steps in afterwards to explain the decision.

This makes instinct both useful and dangerous.

In *Clear Thinking,* Shane Parrish shares a story from psychologist Gary Klein about a paramedic who sensed a heart attack before it was obvious. This kind of rapid pattern recognition can be valuable.

But the same mechanism can also lead to poor decisions when patterns are misread.

Self-awareness allows you to tell the difference.

It also requires understanding the limits of your knowledge. In *Poor Charlie's Almanack*, Charlie Munger recounts the story of Max Planck and his chauffeur. The chauffeur could repeat the lecture, but could not answer deeper questions. This highlights the difference between real understanding and memorisation. Knowing that boundary helps you stay within your circle of competence.

Another part of self-awareness is responsibility. In *Clear Thinking*, Parrish describes being late because his bus did not arrive. His mentor still held him accountable for not planning an alternative. This shifts the focus from blame to control. Without it, it is easy to fall into the self-serving bias, where success is internalised and failure is externalised.

Self-awareness also reveals your default tendencies. The ego can create defensiveness. Social pressure can push you towards the crowd. In *The Black Swan*, Nassim Nicholas Taleb explains how people construct explanations after the fact, even when those explanations were never part of the original decision.

Finally, small actions shape identity over time. In *Atomic Habits*, James Clear explains that each action is a vote for the person you become. Self-awareness allows you to notice those votes as they happen.

This process does not end. As you change, your patterns and beliefs must be revisited. Self-awareness is both a skill and a discipline. It begins with noticing and continues with adjustment.

HOW TO DECIDE

Self-awareness becomes useful when it creates a pause before action.

The goal is not to remove instinct, but to recognise it.

When you feel the urge to act quickly, treat it as a signal to slow down.

Ask simple questions:

- Why am I about to act?
- What happens next if I am wrong?
- Would I make the same decision if I had more time?

Pay attention to repeated outcomes. If the same mistakes appear in different forms, look for the pattern behind them.

Check whether you are acting within your understanding, or just repeating what sounds right.

Take responsibility for your decisions, even when circumstances are not ideal. Focus on what you can control.

Use small actions to shape identity. Each decision reinforces a pattern. Over time, those patterns define how you think and act.

The aim is not perfection, but clarity. Mistakes will still happen, but they will be understood more quickly.

And once a pattern is clearly seen, it becomes harder to follow it blindly.

REFLECTION

What pattern in your behaviour keeps repeating, and what usually happens when you follow it without pausing?

Emotional Discipline

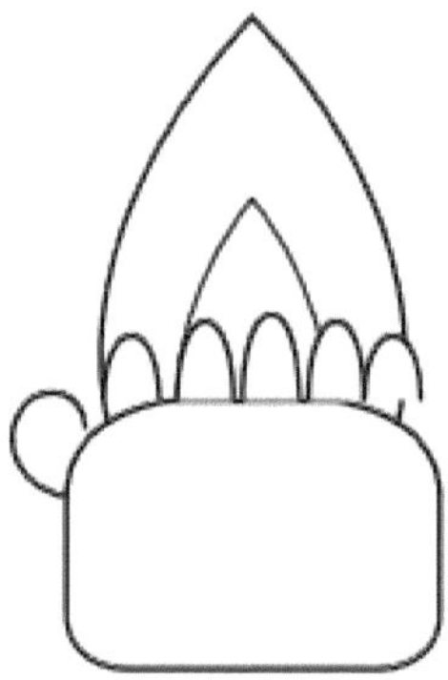

EMOTIONAL DISCIPLINE

act on reason, not reaction

The outcome is decided in the pause before you act.

THE CASE

My early experience with IPO investing in the 1990s followed a familiar pattern. Each new listing carried excitement, strong narratives, and the possibility of quick gains. Decisions were rarely slow or deliberate. They were driven by emotion—mostly greed.

At the time, it did not feel reckless. It felt like opportunity.

Over time, the results made the pattern clear.

The shift did not come from a single insight, but from repeated mistakes. Instead of chasing every new listing, the focus narrowed. Attention moved towards understanding businesses—particularly in familiar sectors like healthcare, chemicals, and parts of consumption. This reduced noise and made decisions more grounded.

Amara Raja was my first multibagger with a meaningful allocation. It also tested my temperament. During the 2006 market correction, the stock fell nearly 50% within 6 weeks. The drop was sharp enough to cause real anxiety. Over the next 6 weeks, it recovered just as quickly. In roughly 3 months, I experienced both extremes.

That episode stayed with me, but it did not change my process. The clearer turning point came later—with Astec Lifesciences.

The IPO, around 2009, was priced at about 80 and rose to nearly 100 on listing. Demand was strong, and there was clear pressure to participate. It was a familiar setup—the kind that had triggered action many times before.

This time was different. No action was taken.

The focus stayed on the business. The company had undertaken significant capital expenditure, which was likely to affect operating profit. Over time, that concern proved correct. By December 2012, the stock had fallen to around 30, where it began to look more reasonable.

The decision to enter came on 12 December 2012 at around 32.

It felt patient. It felt rational. It felt disciplined.

Then the test came.

Within months, the stock dropped sharply to around 13. The move was sudden and uncomfortable. The emotional response was immediate—fear.

This was the second challenge.

The earlier work of understanding the business became critical. The fall did not reflect a change in fundamentals. Despite the discomfort, there was no immediate reaction.

No panic selling.

Looking back, there was even an opportunity to add more at lower levels. Hindsight, of course, is always powerful. Nevertheless, that step was missed. But the key decision was held.

This experience revealed two different pressures:

- The pull of greed when prices rise
- The pressure of fear when prices fall

In both cases, the outcome depended on one thing:

Whether there was a pause before action.

THE REALISATION

The challenge was not predicting the market.

It was managing the reaction to it.

Greed pushed towards action too early. Fear pushed towards action at the worst possible time. Both came from the same place—automatic emotional response.

Discipline does not remove emotion; it prevents it from deciding.

It is about not letting them decide.

The difference between good and poor decisions came down to one small gap:

The space between what happens and what you do next.

THE PRINCIPLE

Discipline is often misunderstood as forcing yourself to act against your desires. In practice, it is something simpler and more precise.

It is the ability to pause between stimulus and response.

In *Clear Thinking*, Shane Parrish explains that much of what we call thinking is actually a fast reaction. These reactions come from built-in mental shortcuts that are quick, automatic, and often emotional. Discipline interrupts these defaults.

This connects closely to *Thinking, Fast and Slow*. Discipline is the habit of allowing the slower system to check the fast one before action is taken.

The well-known bat and ball problem illustrates this clearly. The first answer feels right, but it is wrong because it is not examined. Discipline is choosing to question that first answer.

Emotional discipline follows the same logic. In *Antifragile*, Nassim Nicholas Taleb describes Stoicism as the training of emotional response. The goal is not to eliminate emotion, but to manage it. A simple example is delaying a response when angry. The delay allows emotion to settle and prevents unnecessary damage.

Discipline also includes responsibility. Parrish shares the example of recognising personal patterns and choosing to change them. Awareness alone is not enough. It must be followed by deliberate action.

Environment plays a role as well. In *Atomic Habits*, James Clear explains that disciplined people design their surroundings to reduce temptation. This shifts discipline from effort to structure.

Consistency matters more than intensity. The example of British Cycling under Dave Brailsford shows how small improvements, repeated over time, lead to significant results.

Long-term thinking is another dimension. In *The Most Important Thing*, Howard Marks explains that outcomes can mislead. Good results can come from poor decisions, and bad results can come from sound ones. Discipline requires judging the quality of the process, not just the outcome.

This idea is reinforced in *Behavioural Investing* by James Montier, who highlights the gap between knowing and doing. Discipline closes that gap.

Over time, discipline becomes part of identity. Each action reinforces a pattern. As James Clear explains, habits shape who you become. When those habits are stable, decision-making becomes simpler and more consistent.

Discipline, in the end, is not restriction.

It is a structure that creates clarity.

HOW TO DECIDE

Discipline begins by recognising your first reaction.

When you feel excitement or fear, assume the initial response is automatic. Treat that feeling as a signal to pause.

Ask yourself:

- Am I reacting, or am I choosing?
- What happens if I act immediately?
- What changes if I wait?

If the decision feels urgent, slow down.

Use simple rules instead of relying on willpower:

- If I feel strong emotion → wait

- If I don't understand the situation → don't act
- If I haven't considered what happens next → pause

Reduce unnecessary noise. The more exposure you have to constant information and temptation, the harder discipline becomes.

Focus on process over outcome. Judge decisions by the quality of thinking, not by short-term results.

Take responsibility for your actions. Avoid blaming circumstances. Improvement comes from what you can control.

Over time, repeated behaviour becomes identity. Each disciplined decision makes the next one easier.

The goal is not perfection, but consistency.

Small pauses, repeated over time, lead to better outcomes.

REFLECTION

In this moment, are you reacting—or choosing your response?

Humility

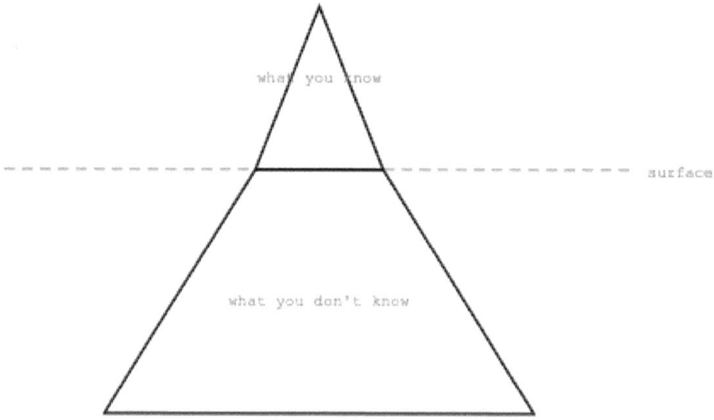

HUMILITY

the unseen dwarfs the seen

The biggest risk is not being wrong—it is being certain you are right.

THE CASE

In 2005, I invested in a company called i-Mate PLC.

At the time, the story was compelling. The company operated in the fast-growing mobile device market. It was listed on AIM at 210 pence, raised around £50 million, and reached a valuation of roughly £232 million. Within a year, that value approached £989 million.

Everything pointed in one direction—growth.

The narrative felt complete. Demand was rising, the market was expanding, and the company appeared well-positioned. It seemed like an opportunity that made sense.

Looking back, the first mistake was already in place.

The business was outside my circle of competence.

Consumer electronics are shaped by rapid change, shifting preferences, and fragile competitive advantages. At the time, this was not fully understood. The company was treated as stable, when in reality it depended heavily on partnerships like HTC—relationships that could change quickly.

But that risk was not visible then.

The story was convincing enough to stop questioning.

As time passed, conditions shifted. Competition increased sharply with the arrival of the iPhone and Android devices. Internal pressures added further strain. The assumptions that once felt solid began to break down.

The response was slow. It took time to accept the loss and exit.

By November 2008, the share price had fallen to around 0.12 pence. The company eventually delisted from AIM and largely ceased operations in 2009.

This was not a failure of access to information.

It was a failure to question what I thought I understood.

THE REALISATION

The problem was not the market.

It was certainty.

The investment was built on a clean, coherent story. But the clarity of the story created confidence that was not supported by real understanding.

What was missing was not intelligence, but humility.

The limits of knowledge were not recognised. Assumptions were not tested. Risks that were not obvious were treated as if they did not exist.

Confidence had drifted away from reality.

Only later did it become clear that the issue was not just the outcome, but the way the decision was made.

THE PRINCIPLE

Humility is not about modesty. It is about seeing clearly.

It begins with accepting that your understanding is always incomplete.

In *The Almanack of Naval Ravikant*, Naval Ravikant describes humans as "monkeys with plans." The point is not to diminish intelligence, but to remind us how easily the ego creates an illusion of control.

This idea is central to what Nassim Taleb calls epistemic humility in *The Black Swan*. We tend to build simple explanations and assume they reflect reality, while ignoring what we cannot see. Humility keeps attention on the unknown as much as the known.

In *Antifragile*, Taleb contrasts this with the "fragilista"—someone who believes they fully understand complex systems.

That confidence leads to fragile decisions because it ignores hidden variables and unintended consequences.

Knowing your limits is a practical expression of humility. Charlie Munger describes this as the circle of competence. Real knowledge includes knowing where your understanding ends—and respecting that boundary.

Humility also shapes how beliefs are held. In *Superforecasting*, Philip Tetlock shows that strong thinkers treat their views as temporary. They expect to be wrong and update quickly when new evidence appears.

This matters because the mind naturally creates confident stories. In *Thinking, Fast and Slow*, Daniel Kahneman explains how we form coherent explanations from limited information. These stories feel complete, even when they are not.

Humility acts as a correction.

It creates distance between belief and certainty.

In practice, this affects behaviour as much as thinking. In *The Psychology of Money*, Morgan Housel argues that behaviour matters more than intelligence. Humility reduces the need to be right or to impress. It creates flexibility, patience, and the ability to learn.

Humility keeps you close to reality.

HOW TO DECIDE

Humility becomes useful when it shapes how you approach decisions.

Start by assuming your view is incomplete.

Ask:

- What might I be missing?
- What would make this wrong?
- What am I assuming without real evidence?

Stay within your circle of competence. Be clear about what you understand and where you are guessing. If key parts of a decision depend on things you cannot assess, reduce exposure or step back.

Be cautious of clean narratives. When something feels simple and convincing, pause. Look for complexity, uncertainty, and opposing views.

Treat beliefs as temporary. Update quickly when new information appears, even if it contradicts your original position.

Separate decisions from ego. Focus on being effective, not being right. If a better idea exists—even if it is not yours—use it.

Finally, judge the process, not just the outcome. A good result does not confirm a good decision, and a bad result does not mean the process was wrong.

Humility keeps you adaptable.

It prevents confidence from turning into overconfidence.

REFLECTION

What might I be missing because I am too confident in my current view?

Independent Thinking

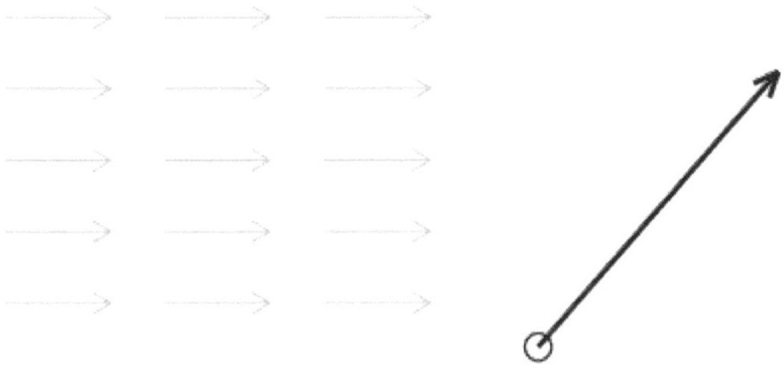

INDEPENDENT THINKING

your own conclusion, not the crowd's

If your thinking feels comfortable, it probably isn't your own.

THE CASE

In mid-2021, Laurus Labs was widely seen as a strong growth story, supported by COVID-related demand.

Then the narrative changed.

As that demand faded, revenues and margins dropped sharply. Institutional sentiment turned negative. Many investors followed, and the stock was largely avoided.

The prevailing view was simple:

The company had benefited from a temporary tailwind, and its best days were behind it.

It was a clean, widely accepted story.

That was the first signal to pause.

The reaction in the market reflected what Howard Marks describes as first-level thinking. It focused on what had already happened and assumed the trend would continue.

Looking deeper required stepping away from that narrative.

A CDMO business is not defined by short-term revenue. Its value comes from underlying capabilities—pivoting, regulatory approvals, scientific expertise, and manufacturing capacity. These take years to build and are not easily replaced.

At the time, the company had expanded capacity significantly and built a growing pipeline of projects. It had passed multiple regulatory inspections and was moving into new areas.

These details were visible. The long-term earnings power was improving, even as current earnings remained weak. Instant gratification reads well in theory, but rarely holds in practice.

Many negative opinions sounded confident, but did not fully engage with how the business actually worked. This echoed an idea from *Poor Charlie's Almanack*—the difference between repeating information and truly understanding it.

The key question was not what had just happened.

It was what would happen next as capacity began to be utilised.

Taking this view was uncomfortable.

The price did not immediately reflect it. The broader sentiment remained negative. There was no quick validation.

But the situation was not one-sided.

A more flexible, "fox-like" perspective—described by Philip Tetlock in *Superforecasting*—helped balance the picture. Revenues had declined, but the pipeline was strengthening. EBITDA margins were under pressure, yet the core business remained intact, with gross margins gradually improving.

Over time, the market adjusted.

The stock rose significantly from its lows.

For most investors, the near-term outcome matters more than the process.

The opportunity was visible—but only if you stepped away from the obvious conclusion.

THE REALISATION

The challenge was not a lack of information.

It was the pull of consensus.

When a view is widely shared and feels simple, it becomes easy to accept it without questioning. An agreement creates the illusion of correctness.

Independent thinking begins at that point.

It requires asking whether the conclusion is actually true, or just widely repeated.

The difficulty is not intellectual.

It is psychological—and social.

Going against the crowd creates discomfort. There is doubt, and often no immediate confirmation. But without that discomfort, thinking remains shallow.

THE PRINCIPLE

Independent thinking is the ability to examine reality for yourself—not to oppose the crowd, but to avoid relying on it.

Most thinking is automatic. In *Thinking, Fast and Slow*, Daniel Kahneman shows how quickly the mind jumps to conclusions. The first answer often feels right, even when it is not. Independent thinking requires slowing down and checking that instinct.

One way to do this is through first principles. In *The Almanack of Naval Ravikant*, Naval Ravikant emphasises building understanding from basic truths rather than accepting inherited beliefs. This approach is slower, but it leads to clearer reasoning.

True understanding is different from repetition. The story of Max Planck's chauffeur, shared in *Poor Charlie's Almanack*, highlights this distinction. Being able to repeat an idea is not the same as being able to think with it.

Independent thinking also requires flexibility. In *Superforecasting*, Philip Tetlock contrasts "hedgehogs," who rely on a single idea, with "foxes," who adapt as new information appears. Better judgement comes from updating views, not defending them.

It also involves thinking beyond the obvious. Howard Marks describes the difference between first-level and second-level thinking. Most people focus on immediate outcomes. Independent thinkers ask what happens next and what others might be missing.

This often means standing apart. As Warren Buffett has noted, being right does not depend on agreement, but on reasoning and evidence.

Over time, this mindset builds responsibility. You are no longer relying on others to form your views. Mistakes become part of learning, and thinking becomes more precise.

Independent thinking is not about being different for its own sake.

It is about being deliberate.

HOW TO DECIDE

Independent thinking starts when something feels obvious.

Pause and ask:

- Is this conclusion based on evidence or repetition?
- Am I thinking, or am I agreeing?

Break the situation down to basic truths. Focus on what is actually happening, not just how it is being socially described.

Separate facts from interpretation.

Actively consider the opposing view. If you cannot explain it clearly, your understanding is incomplete.

Think beyond the present. Ask:

- What happens next?
- What is the second-order effect?
- What might the market be missing?

Be prepared for discomfort. Even with sound reasoning, you may be early—or alone—for a period of time.

Treat outcomes as feedback. If you are wrong, adjust. If you are right, understand why. Avoid rushing to conclusions; some business cycles take time to play out.

In capital-intensive businesses like CDMO, lead indicators of quality—especially people—and execution matter. They should not be ignored.

The goal is not to oppose the crowd.

It is to think clearly, regardless of what the crowd believes.

REFLECTION

Am I thinking this through from first principles—or simply accepting what feels obvious?

The Long Game

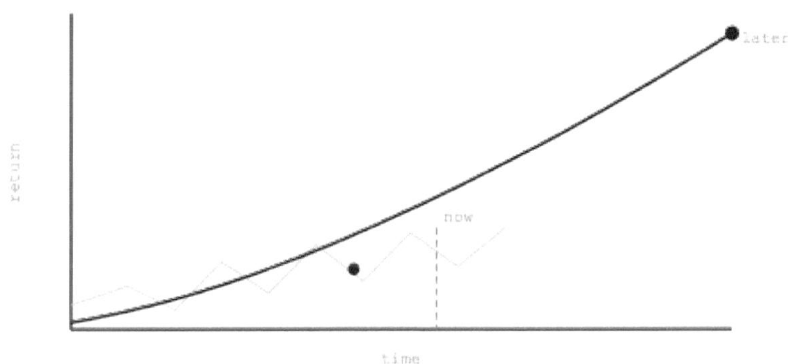

THE LONG GAME

time rewards patience, not noise

Compounding feels slow—until it suddenly doesn't.

THE CASE

For a long time, progress did not feel like progress.

Effort was being made—reading, analysing, tracking businesses—but the results were not always visible. Returns were inconsistent. Some decisions worked, others did not. There was no clear sense of compounding.

It felt slow.

At times, it felt like nothing was happening at all.

This is where most people change direction.

The temptation is always to look for faster results—to switch strategies, chase momentum, or react to short-term outcomes. The discomfort lies in the gap between effort and visible reward.

Over time, a different pattern began to emerge.

The focus shifted away from quick outcomes and towards businesses capable of compounding over long periods. Companies such as Amara Raja, Atul, RPG Life, JB Pharma, Praj Industries, Neuland Labs, Navin Fluorine, Deepak Nitrite, Laurus Labs, and Narayana Health reflected this shift.

There were periods of significant drawdowns. Declines of 60–70% are deeply uncomfortable. They are easy to read about, but far harder to endure in real time, as the losses unfold day after day.

These were not driven by short-term narratives.

They had:

- reinvestment opportunities
- capable management
- improving economics over time

Holding them required patience.

There were periods where prices stagnated or declined. There were phases where nothing seemed to be happening. But underneath, the businesses were evolving—capacity expanding, margins improving, capabilities strengthening.

The results did not appear immediately.

But when they did, they appeared all at once.

Looking back, what felt like sudden gains were not sudden at all. They were the result of decisions made years earlier.

The real challenge was not finding opportunities.

It was staying with them long enough.

THE REALISATION

The problem was not a lack of effort.

It was the expectation of immediate results.

Progress in the long game is uneven. Most of the time, nothing appears to change. Then, over a short period, everything does.

This creates a psychological trap.

When results are delayed, it feels like the approach is not working. That feeling leads to change—often at exactly the wrong time.

The insight is simple, but difficult to live:

Time does not reward activity. It rewards consistency.

It rewards consistency applied to the right things.

Patience is not passive.

It is the decision to continue without immediate validation.

THE PRINCIPLE

The long game is built on compounding.

Small, consistent actions—applied over time—lead to outcomes that appear disproportionate to the effort. But this process is not linear.

In *Atomic Habits*, James Clear describes the "Valley of Disappointment." Progress often remains invisible until a threshold is crossed, like an ice cube that does not melt until the temperature rises enough. What appears sudden is usually accumulated effort finally becoming visible.

This requires deep patience.

It means continuing even when there is no visible progress. What is often called overnight success is simply the delayed return of long-term effort.

Focus is essential. In *The Almanack of Naval Ravikant*, Naval suggests playing long-term games with long-term people. Compounding strengthens when trust, alignment, and time work together.

The shift from goals to systems reinforces this idea. Goals define outcomes, but systems define behaviour. Systems create consistency, which allows compounding to take place even when motivation fluctuates.

Long-term thinking also requires depth. Howard Marks describes second-level thinking as looking beyond immediate outcomes to understand what happens next. This often means accepting short-term discomfort for long-term benefit.

But patience only works when applied to quality.

Time does not fix weak foundations. In investing, poor economics do not improve simply with time.

Strong management, however, can compound value by transforming weak businesses into more sustainable ones.

Both RPG Life and JB Pharma were low-quality businesses around 2014, with weak margins. By the time I exited, they had become sought after, with valuation re-rating alone contributing more than 10x over a decade of holding.

People play a central role in this. In *The Intelligent Investor*, Benjamin Graham introduces Mr. Market to show that price and value can diverge. What matters is the underlying strength of the business and the discipline of those running it.

Alignment strengthens outcomes. In *Skin in the Game*, Nassim Nicholas Taleb explains that decision-makers who share risk behave more responsibly. Similarly, in *Principles*, Ray Dalio shows how trust builds through consistent behaviour over time.

At its core, the long game is simple:

Choose carefully. Stay consistent. Allow time to work.

HOW TO DECIDE

Start by choosing where to play.

You cannot apply patience to everything. Focus on a few areas where effort can compound over time.

Check the quality of what you are committing to:

- Is the foundation strong?
- Will this improve with time, or decay?

If the underlying quality is weak, patience will not help.

Pay close attention to people. Look for long-term thinking, aligned incentives, and consistent behaviour. Trust builds through actions over time, not words.

Shift from goals to systems:

- What daily or repeated actions will drive progress?
- Can you sustain them even when results are not visible?

Think beyond the present:

- What happens next?
- What does this look like in 3–5 years?

Be willing to accept short-term discomfort if the long-term direction is sound.

Protect your ability to stay in the game. Avoid decisions that can cause permanent damage. Compounding only works if you remain in place long enough.

Be selective. Say no often. Like waiting for the right pitch, discipline improves outcomes.

Stay flexible. If the underlying reality changes, adjust. Patience should not become stubbornness.

The goal is not constant activity.

It is consistent progress.

REFLECTION

Am I committing my time and energy to something that is truly worth compounding over the long term?

Risk Management

You don't need to be right—you need to survive being wrong.

THE CASE

Risk rarely feels like risk at the time you take it.

It usually feels like opportunity.

In April 2020, during the first wave of COVID, I invested in Narayana Health.

The environment was dominated by fear and uncertainty. Hospitals were not seen as obvious beneficiaries, and the sector did not carry a strong history of wealth creation in India. There was little excitement built into the stock.

The company was trading at around 10–12 times earnings, below earlier (post-IPO) levels.

What stood out was not the short-term situation, but the underlying business—its cost structure, scale, and leadership under Devi Shetty and his family. There was clear, measurable skin in the game.

The earnings transcripts were consistent and convincing. Narayana was playing the long game, and long-term demand for healthcare remained intact.

The position was meaningful, but carefully sized.

There was no certainty about outcomes. The focus was on ensuring that if things went wrong, the damage would be limited.

Over time, the market reassessed the sector, and the stock performed strongly.

A different kind of experience came from Praj Industries.

The investment began in 2014 at around ₹40. For years, there was little progress. By the time COVID arrived, the stock was only around ₹55. It felt slow. It felt unproductive.

Holding required patience.

Each time the position was reviewed, the same factors remained:

- a net cash balance sheet
- consistent operating cash flow
- dividend payments
- a long-term thesis around industrial biotechnology and biofuels

The risk of permanent damage appeared low.

The challenge was not a downside.

It was time.

Eventually, the stock rose significantly, reaching around ₹800.

The outcome was not driven by timing, but by staying in the position long enough for the underlying value to emerge.

These two experiences looked different on the surface.

But they shared the same foundation:

The focus was not on predicting what would happen.

It was on ensuring survival while staying exposed to opportunity.

THE REALISATION

The biggest risk is *not* volatility.

It is *ruin*.

Losses can be recovered. Time can correct mistakes. But some outcomes remove you from the game entirely.

That is where risk management begins.

The mistake most people make is trying to predict the future.

The future is uncertain and often behaves in ways that are not just unknown but unknowable.

The better approach is different:

Instead of asking *"What will happen?"*

Ask *"What happens if I am wrong?"*

Risk is not about being correct. It is about *surviving* being wrong.

THE PRINCIPLE

Risk management is not about avoiding risk.

It is about choosing which risks to take and ensuring they do not destroy you.

In *The Black Swan*, Nassim Nicholas Taleb uses the story of a turkey that feels safe until an unexpected event changes everything. A long history of stability does not protect against rare, extreme outcomes.

This is why prediction is unreliable.

In *Antifragile*, Taleb explains that systems built only on past data can fail when exposed to larger shocks. Reality contains hidden risks that are not visible in normal conditions.

The focus, therefore, shifts from prediction to resilience.

In *The Intelligent Investor*, Ben Graham introduces the idea of a margin of safety—a buffer that allows for error. The goal is not to be right every time, but to survive being wrong.

Howard Marks reinforces this with the idea that risk lies in extremes, not averages. A situation may appear safe on average, but still contain the potential for serious damage.

Other principles support this:

- **Redundancy** (Taleb): having more than you need to absorb shocks
- **Process over outcome** (Michael Mauboussin, Shane Parrish): avoiding false confidence from lucky results

- **Skin in the game** (Taleb): aligning decisions with consequences

At a personal level, the rule is simple.

As Naval Ravikant emphasises, you must avoid risks that *remove* you from the game entirely.

Because compounding only works if you survive long enough.

How to Decide

Start by assuming you are wrong.

Ask:

- What could go wrong here?
- If it does, how much damage will it cause?
- Can I recover?

Look for a margin of safety—and asymmetry:

- Is there a buffer against error?
- Is the downside limited and the upside meaningful?

Focus on survival:

- Avoid situations that can cause permanent loss
- Avoid concentration that can destroy your ability to continue

Separate outcome from process:

- Was the decision sound, regardless of the result?
- Would you make the same decision again under similar conditions?

Pay attention to structure:

- Can you size positions appropriately?
- Can you combine safety with selective risk (barbell approach)?

Check alignment:

- Do decision-makers have skin in the game?
- Are incentives aligned with long-term outcomes?

Be patient:

- Good decisions often take time to play out
- Avoid reacting to short-term volatility

Finally, manage yourself:

- Fear and greed distort risk perception
- The biggest mistakes often come from emotional reactions under stress

The goal is not to eliminate uncertainty.

It is important to choose which uncertainties you can live with.

REFLECTION

If this decision turns out to be wrong, will I still be able to continue and recover?

MOVEMENT II – WHERE THINKING BREAKS

Overconfidence Bias

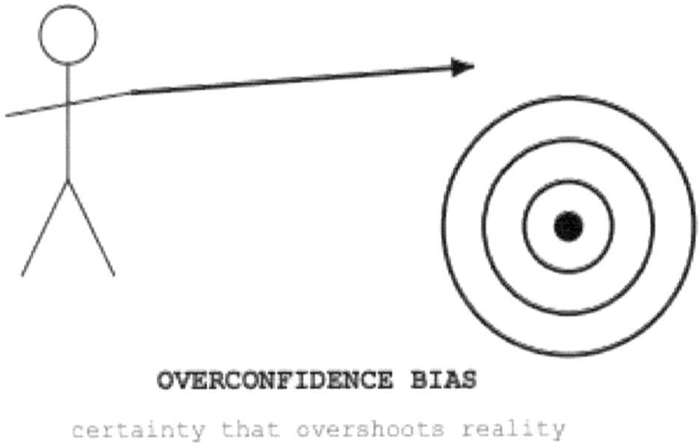

Clarity is often the feeling you get just before you stop checking.

THE CASE

In markets, overconfidence rarely feels like a mistake.

It feels like clarity.

The rise of Super Micro Computer is a good example.

The stock surged rapidly on the back of AI excitement. The story was simple and compelling: increasing demand for AI infrastructure, strong positioning, and visible growth. Everything appeared aligned.

The narrative made sense.

That was the problem.

As the price rose, confidence followed. The story was repeated, reinforced, and widely accepted. Few questioned whether the assumptions behind it were solid.

Warning signs began to appear:

- Concerns raised by Hindenburg Research
- Accounting-related issues
- Resignation of its auditor

At the same time, financial signals were becoming harder to ignore:

- Rising debt
- Volatile cash flows
- Heavy inventory build-up based on continued demand

These were not minor details.

They suggested that the future depended on multiple things going right at once.

But the dominant narrative did not change.

The visible story, AI growth, remained strong. Less visible risks were pushed aside.

When reality eventually caught up, the stock fell sharply, wiping out significant value.

The issue was not a lack of information.

It was selective attention.

Confidence had drifted away from evidence.

THE REALISATION

Overconfidence does not come from knowing too much.

It comes from *feeling certain too quickly.*

When a story is clear and widely accepted, it creates the illusion of understanding. Agreement reinforces that illusion. The more people believe something, the more it feels true.

But clarity is not the same as correctness.

The real danger is not being wrong. It is stopping the check.

THE PRINCIPLE

Overconfidence bias is the tendency to overestimate what we know, how good we are, and how accurate our judgement is.

In *Thinking, Fast and Slow*, Daniel Kahneman shows how easily this happens. The bat and ball problem demonstrates how quickly we accept an intuitive answer without checking it. The mistake is not complexity—it is the absence of pause.

Psychologists describe overconfidence in three forms:

- **Overestimation**: believing we are better than we are
- **Overplacement**: believing we are better than others
- **Overprecision**: being too certain about our knowledge

Together, they create a false sense of certainty.

Kahneman also introduces *WYSIATI*—'what you see is all there is'. The mind builds coherent stories from limited information and ignores what is missing. If the story feels complete, we trust it.

This creates an illusion of understanding.

Confidence grows not because knowledge is strong, but because the narrative is smooth.

Even experts are not immune. In *Superforecasting*, Philip Tetlock finds that many experts perform no better than chance. As confidence increases, flexibility often decreases.

This extends to personal experience. In *The Psychology of Money*, Morgan Housel notes that success can be a poor teacher. Good outcomes reinforce confidence, even when they result partly from luck.

Over time, this leads to a dangerous pattern:

Confidence replaces curiosity.

And once questioning stops, mistakes compound.

HOW TO DECIDE

Overconfidence is hardest to detect when it feels strongest.

So, start with a simple rule:

If something feels obvious, pause.

Ask:

- What evidence supports this?
- What might I be missing?
- What assumptions am I making?

Separate facts from interpretation. A clear story is not enough—check whether it is complete.

Count your assumptions:

- How many things need to go right?
- What happens if one of them fails?

Look at the outside view:

- What happened in similar situations?
- How often do these stories actually work out?

Actively challenge your own thinking. As Charlie Munger suggests, be able to argue the opposite side clearly.

Use practical tools:

- **Premortem** (Gary Klein): assume failure and ask why
- **Decision diary** (James Montier): record reasoning and review outcomes

Focus on expectations:

- What is already priced in?
- Does success depend on perfection?

Think in probabilities, not certainties. Update your view as new information appears, rather than defending your original position.

The goal is not to eliminate confidence.

It is to make sure it is earned.

REFLECTION

Am I trusting a clear story—or have I tested what might be missing?

Anchoring Bias

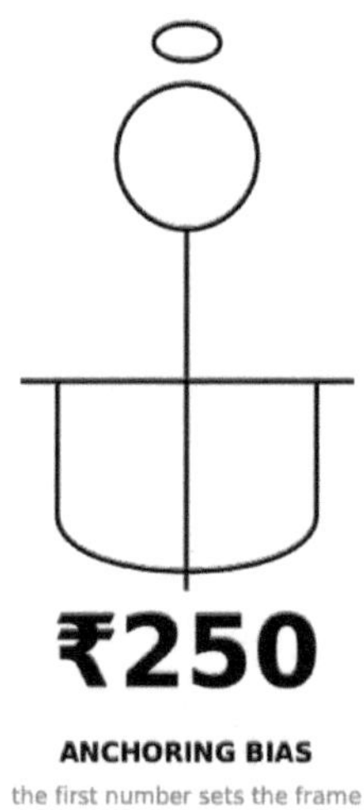

The first number you see quietly shapes everything that follows.

THE CASE

In 2021, Clean Science and Technology was listed at around 33 times price-to-sales.

That number became the starting point.

From there, discussions did not begin with value. They began with a comparison. Was it slightly expensive? Slightly cheap? Should it be 30 times or 35 times?

Very few stepped back to ask whether the starting point itself made sense.

As the stock rose, the anchor moved.

Valuations reached around 53 times sales and 42 times price-to-book. These new levels began to feel justified. The narrative supported them—quality business, strong growth, limited supply. The numbers no longer felt extreme because they had become familiar.

Then the cycle turned.

By 2025, valuations had fallen to around 17 times sales.

Reactions still depended on the earlier anchors.

Some investors saw value because the stock had "halved" from its peak. Others remained attached to the original growth narrative and expected a return to previous levels.

In both cases, judgement was shaped by the past—not by present reality.

The key question was no longer:

What is this worth today?

It had quietly become:

How does this compare to what it used to be?

THE REALISATION

The problem was not the number itself.

It was the starting point.

Once a reference is set, thinking begins to orbit around it. Even when new information appears, adjustments are small. The original anchor continues to shape what feels reasonable.

The most subtle effect is this:

Anchors move.

What once seemed extreme becomes normal. What once felt expensive becomes a benchmark. Over time, perception shifts without being noticed.

The danger is not just being influenced.

It is forgetting that you are being influenced.

THE PRINCIPLE

Anchoring bias is the tendency to rely too heavily on the first piece of information we encounter.

Instead of judging something independently, we adjust our thinking around that starting point.

In *Thinking, Fast and Slow,* Daniel Kahneman describes anchoring as one of the most robust findings in psychology. Even when the initial number is random or clearly irrelevant, it still affects judgement.

This happens through two mechanisms:

- **Deliberate adjustment**: we try to move away from the anchor, but not far enough
- **Automatic influence (priming)**: the number shapes what feels reasonable without conscious awareness

The mind prefers comparison over absolute judgement, and that is where error begins.

Once an anchor exists, thinking becomes relative.

This effect is powerful and persistent. Kahneman and Amos Tversky demonstrated that even random numbers—like those from a wheel of fortune—can influence estimates about unrelated topics.

Anchoring also appears in behaviour, not just numbers. In *The Almanack of Naval Ravikant*, Naval points out that identity itself can become anchored. Past habits create fixed beliefs about who we are, limiting change.

In decision-making, anchoring often works together with the 'inside view'. As Philip Tetlock explains in *Superforecasting*, we rely on our own narrative instead of looking at how similar situations typically unfold.

Anchors reinforce that narrative.

They make the story feel grounded even when it is not.

HOW TO DECIDE

Anchoring cannot be removed, but it can be weakened.

Start by questioning the starting point:

- Where did this number come from?
- Is it relevant, or just the first thing I saw?

If the answer feels obvious, pause.

Rebuild your judgement from scratch:

- What would I think if I had never seen this number?
- What is the value based on fundamentals, not history?

Avoid relying on past prices:

- A stock being down 50% does not make it cheap

- A stock being up does not make it expensive

Focus on what it is worth now and what it can become.

Use the outside view:

- How do similar businesses get valued?
- What typically happens in comparable situations?

Actively challenge the anchor:

- What if the true value is far below this number?
- What if it is far above?

Good systems help reduce bias. As James Clear suggests, structured processes reduce reliance on instinct. Use multiple sources, independent analysis, and clear frameworks.

Watch for non-numeric anchors as well:

- “This is a great company.”
- “This always works.”
- “This is how I am.”

These can be just as limiting as price anchors.

The goal is not to eliminate anchors.

It is to stop them from defining your judgement.

REFLECTION

Am I judging this based on its true value or just reacting to where it started?

The Crowd and the Moment

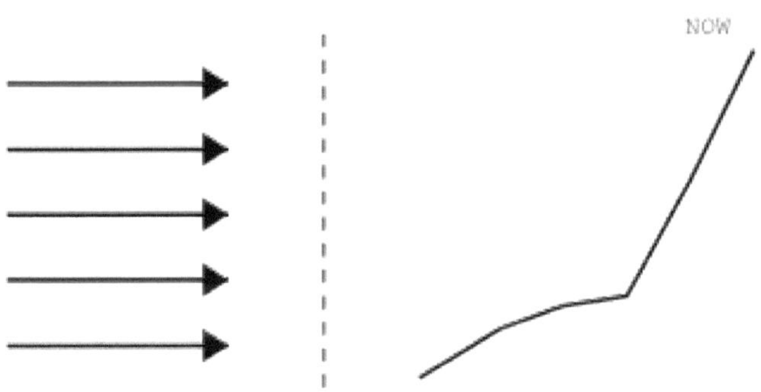

THE CROWD AND THE MOMENT

herding & recency bias

The crowd feels safest exactly when it is most wrong.

THE CASE

During COVID, markets offered a clear example of how the crowd and recent events shape decisions.

Diagnostic companies like Dr Lal PathLabs and Metropolis Healthcare saw rapid growth as testing demand surged.

The story was simple:

- Demand was rising.
- Revenues were strong.
- Visibility looked high.

Prices followed.

As valuations increased—reaching around 15 times sales—more investors joined. The logic felt reinforced. If everyone was buying, it seemed safe to follow.

At the same time, hospital companies like Narayana Health and Apollo Hospitals were out of favour.

Their recent performance looked weak. The narrative was unclear. The crowd stayed away.

But the underlying reality had not changed.

Long-term demand for healthcare remained intact. The difference was not in fundamentals—it was in perception.

The crowd was reacting to what was visible:

- Recent growth in diagnostics
- Recent weakness in hospitals

What had just happened was treated as what would continue.

Over time, that assumption was corrected.

The key insight was not which sector performed better.

It was how quickly perception followed the crowd and how strongly it followed recent events.

THE REALISATION

The problem was not a lack of information.

It was the weight given to what was immediate.

When many people act in the same way, it creates a sense of validation. When something has worked recently, it feels more likely to keep working.

Together, these forces are powerful.

The crowd answers the question:

"What are others doing?"

Recency answers:

"What has just worked?"

Neither answers:

"What is actually true?"

That gap is where mistakes happen.

THE PRINCIPLE

Much of human behaviour is shaped by mental shortcuts developed for survival.

Two of the strongest are herding and recency bias.

Herding is the tendency to follow others. In *Atomic Habits*, James Clear explains that we copy the close, the many, and the powerful. This helped survival in the past, but today it can lead to unexamined decisions.

Recency bias is the tendency to overweight recent events. In *Thinking, Fast and Slow*, Daniel Kahneman shows how vivid and recent information feels more important than it really is.

Together, they create a reinforcing loop:

- The crowd moves

- Recent success confirms the movement
- More people follow

This can drive trends far beyond what fundamentals justify.

Classic experiments highlight this. In *Influence: The Psychology of Persuasion*, Robert Cialdini describes Solomon Asch's experiments, where people agreed with a group even when the answer was clearly wrong.

Even experts are affected. As Michael Mauboussin notes in *More Than You Know*, systems that rely on imitation can collapse when feedback loops reinforce the wrong behaviour.

Recency bias adds another layer. In *Antifragile*, Taleb describes how people assume recent experience defines what is possible. Similarly, in *The Psychology of Money*, Morgan Housel explains that personal experience shapes perception, even when it represents only a small part of reality.

The result is predictable:

We follow what others are doing.

We expect what just happened to continue.

And we mistake both for truth.

HOW TO DECIDE

Start by recognising when the crowd is strongest.

If everyone agrees, pause.

Ask:

- What is the crowd seeing?
- What might it be missing?

Separate recent from structural:

- Is this temporary, or is it lasting?

- What has actually changed and what has not?

Reverse the perspective:

- What could go wrong here?
- What would make this trend fail?

This follows the idea of inversion, often used by Charlie Munger.

Check independence:

- Would I make this decision if no one else were doing it?

If the answer is no, the decision may not be your own.

Slow down when urgency is highest. Rising trends create fear of missing out. Falling trends create fear of loss. Both push towards action without reflection.

Step back from the environment when needed. Distance reduces the pull of the crowd.

Focus on the future:

- What needs to happen for this to work?
- How likely is that outcome?

The crowd focuses on what is happening now.

Better decisions come from thinking about what happens next.

REFLECTION

What would I choose if I ignored what everyone else is doing and focused only on the underlying reality?

Narrative Fallacy

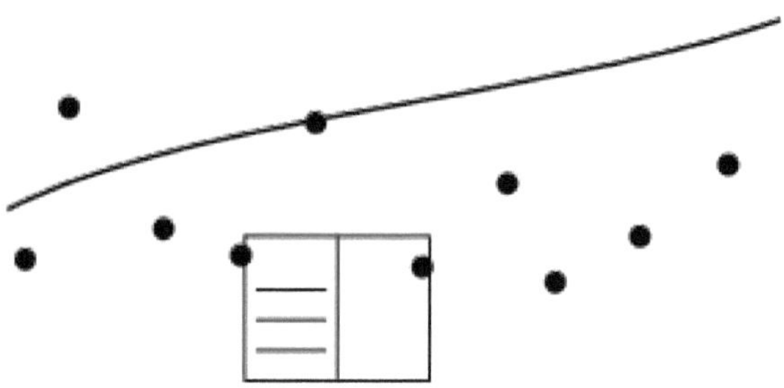

NARRATIVE FALLACY

the story we tell over the truth

A good story feels like truth—even when it isn't.

THE CASE

In 2015, Syngene International was often described as the "WuXi of India."

It was a powerful idea.

The comparison to WuXi AppTec suggested a clear path:

- move from research into manufacturing
- build an integrated platform
- compound growth over time

The story was simple, logical and easy to repeat. I found it convincing.

"We have a high single-digit number of assets that we are supporting our partners with in late-stage clinical development—Phase 2b or 3—and we have three long-term commercial supply arrangements in place."

—Syngene's first earnings call post listing

The narrative filled in gaps that were not yet proven. It pointed to a future that felt realistic—because it had already worked elsewhere.

But the underlying reality was less clear.

Key concerns remained:

- The manufacturing scale was still developing
- Revenue breakdowns were not fully visible
- The IPO did not raise fresh capital for that transition

These were important uncertainties.

But they were easy to overlook.

The story felt complete.

Over time, that gap became visible.

Years later—more clearly after 2023 and into 2024—the business still looked primarily like a CRO. The manufacturing transition had not evolved as expected. The original narrative had moved ahead of reality.

The conclusion was not that the business was poor.

It was that the story had been too certain.

A similar pattern appeared in another situation.

In the case of Cohance Lifesciences, management communication consistently reinforced a single narrative of growth. They signalled $1 billion in revenue by 2030 and $2 billion by 2035 with confidence.

When results weakened in FY26:

- Revenue declines were described as 'timing'.
- Zero contribution from segments was seen as 'bottoming out'.
- Delays became 'phasing'.

Each data point was absorbed into the same story.

The narrative remained intact—even as reality became less clear.

This is how narrative fallacy works in practice.

The story does not break.

It adapts.

THE REALISATION

The problem was not the story itself.

It was the certainty it created.

Stories compress complexity and hide uncertainty. They make the world easier to understand. But in doing so, they remove uncertainty, hide missing information and create confidence that may not be justified.

The mind prefers a clear explanation over an incomplete truth.

Once a narrative takes hold:

- new information is fitted into it
- contradictions are explained away
- uncertainty is reduced artificially

The danger is not being wrong. It is becoming certain too early.

It is becoming too confident in a story that has not been fully tested.

THE PRINCIPLE

The narrative fallacy is the tendency to create coherent stories to explain events even when those stories are incomplete or incorrect.

In *The Black Swan*, Taleb explains that we turn complex reality into simple cause-and-effect explanations. These stories are easier to remember and feel more meaningful, but they often hide randomness and uncertainty.

A simple illustration comes from E. M. Forster in *Aspects of the Novel*:

- "The king died, and the queen died" → fact
- "The king died, and the queen died of grief" → story

The second feels better because it adds causality, even if that causality is imagined.

This instinct is reinforced by how the mind works. We build a complete story from available information and fail to ask what is missing.

Memory adds another distortion. Hindsight bias makes outcomes feel predictable after they occur. As Michael Mauboussin explains, we become "Monday morning quarterbacks", rewriting the past to match the outcome.

Narratives also shape interpretation in real time. In *Behavioural Investing*, James Montier shows that people are more convinced by the same facts when presented as a coherent story rather than in random order.

Even expertise does not protect against this. In *Superforecasting*, Philip Tetlock finds that confident narratives often lead to poor predictions because they resist updating.

Taleb's "green lumber" fallacy adds another layer. People can understand a story perfectly and still miss what actually drives outcomes. Theory can feel right while reality behaves differently.

The result is a consistent pattern:

Stories create understanding.

Understanding creates confidence.

Confidence reduces questioning.

HOW TO DECIDE

Stories are useful, but they must be tested.

Start by separating facts from explanation:

- What actually happened?
- What is being assumed about why it happened?

Ask what is missing:

- What information is not visible?
- What would weaken this story?

Be cautious of smooth narratives:

- Does everything fit too neatly?
- Are contradictions being explained away too easily?

Watch how new information is handled:

- Is it challenging the story?
- Or being absorbed into it?

Use the outside view:

- How do similar situations usually unfold?
- How often does this kind of story actually work?

Write down your reasoning at the time of decision. This helps avoid hindsight bias and shows whether your thinking was sound or reconstructed later.

Separate understanding from execution:

- Is this idea proven in practice?
- Or just logical in theory?

Be especially careful when:

- valuation is high
- expectations are strong
- communication is consistently optimistic

These conditions increase the pressure to maintain the story.

The goal is not to reject narratives.

It is to hold them lightly.

REFLECTION

What part of this story feels convincing but rests on assumptions I have not properly tested?

Loss Aversion

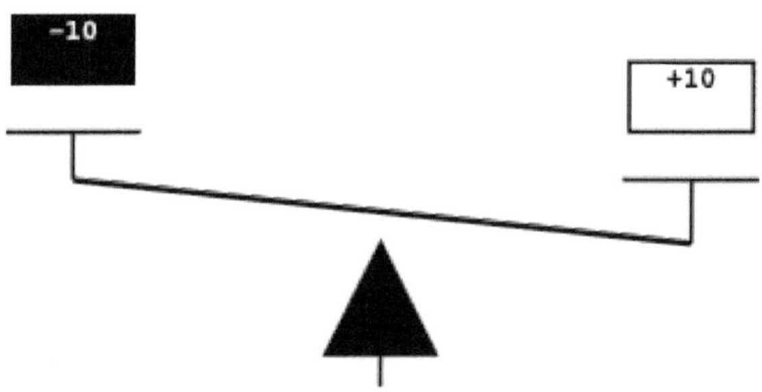

LOSS AVERSION

losses sting more than gains please

We avoid small losses and walk into bigger ones.

THE CASE

Loss aversion is easiest to see where decisions feel personal. Healthcare provides a clear example.

Consider the recent rise of GLP-1 medications such as **Wegovy** or **Ozempic**.

These treatments can produce meaningful long-term benefits—weight loss, improved metabolic health, and reduced risk of future disease.

Yet many eligible patients hesitate to begin.

A patient who feels relatively well today is asked to accept immediate trade-offs:

- side effects such as nausea
- the burden of ongoing injections
- cost and commitment

These are experiences now, and they feel like losses.

The benefits, by contrast, are delayed and uncertain. Weight loss is gradual. Risk reduction is invisible. The future improvement cannot be directly felt.

So the decision becomes unbalanced:

- a certain short-term loss (discomfort, effort, cost)
- versus a probable long-term gain (better health)

Many choose to do nothing.

The same pattern appears after treatment begins. Some patients discontinue early because the initial side effects outweigh the benefits they have not yet experienced. Others, once progress is made, become reluctant to stop—because stopping feels like losing what has been gained.

Avoiding change works in both directions:

- not starting avoids an immediate loss
- not stopping avoids a future loss

Doctors face similar pressures. Prescribing a new therapy involves uncertainty. Changing course later can feel like admitting the initial decision may not have been optimal. As a result, staying the course often feels safer—even when new evidence suggests a better alternative.

This behaviour is not irrational.

It is consistent.

The same pattern appears in investing:

- Holding losing stocks to 'get back to cost'
- Selling winners too early to lock in gains
- Taking bigger risks after losses to recover quickly

In each case, the decision is shaped less by value and more by how gains and losses are *felt*.

THE REALISATION

The problem is not loss itself.

It is how loss is experienced.

Losses feel heavier than gains.

That imbalance distorts decisions:

- We avoid small losses even when they lead to larger gains
- We accept large risks to avoid recognising a loss
- We hold on to the past instead of focusing on the future

The key insight is simple:

A loss is not just an outcome.

It is a feeling, and that feeling drives behaviour.

Unless that is recognised, decisions will be guided by emotion rather than logic.

THE PRINCIPLE

Loss aversion is the tendency for losses to feel more painful than equivalent gains feel rewarding.

In *Thinking, Fast and Slow*, Daniel Kahneman explains that losses are typically felt about twice as strongly as gains.

This comes from evolution. Missing an opportunity was manageable. Failing to avoid danger could be fatal. Over time, the brain became more sensitive to threats than rewards.

This bias operates through a **'reference' point**.

We judge outcomes relative to where we are now, not in absolute terms. The same result can feel like a gain or a loss depending on the starting point.

It also connects to several related behaviours:

- **Disposition effect**: selling winners too early, holding losers too long
- **Endowment effect** (described by James Montier): ownership increases perceived value
- **Sunk cost fallacy**: continuing because of past investment, even when it no longer makes sense

Loss aversion also changes risk-taking:

- When facing gains → people become conservative
- When facing losses → people become risk-seeking

This explains why small losses can lead to big mistakes.

In *Fooled by Randomness,* Nassim Taleb shows how frequent feedback intensifies this effect. Small losses, seen often, feel overwhelming even when long-term outcomes are positive.

The result is a consistent distortion:

We protect against short-term pain even when it harms long-term outcomes.

HOW TO DECIDE

Start by separating feeling from reality.

When something feels like a loss, pause and ask:

- Is this a real loss—or just discomfort?
- Does it matter in the long term?

Identify your reference point:

- Am I anchored to a past price or decision?
- Would I make the same choice today from scratch?

Use a simple test:

- If I did not own this, would I buy it now?

If not, holding may be driven by loss aversion.

Avoid reacting to recover losses:

- Do not take bigger risks just to 'get back'
- Accept small losses early to avoid larger ones later

Reduce noise:

- Avoid checking outcomes too frequently
- Focus on long-term progress, not short-term fluctuations

Reframe decisions:

- What is the expected outcome from here, not from the past?
- What is the cost of doing nothing?

Accept that some discomfort is necessary:

- Good decisions often feel bad in the short term
- Avoiding discomfort can lead to worse outcomes

The goal is not to eliminate loss aversion.

It is important to recognise when it is driving your decision.

REFLECTION

What part of this decision feels like a loss—but may not matter in the long run?

MOVEMENT III – THE BRIDGE

The Limits of Rational Thinking

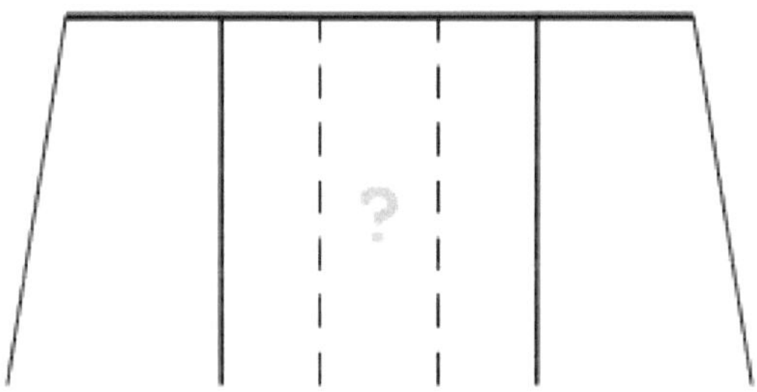

THE LIMITS OF RATIONAL THINKING

where logic runs out

Knowing better is easy—doing better is the problem.

We like to think of ourselves as rational people who make decisions through clear logic. But that is not how the mind works. Most thoughts and impressions appear in consciousness without us knowing where they came from.

The brain is, in many ways, a prediction machine—constantly seeking the easiest path to an answer. This creates a problem: conscious attention is limited and can focus on only one thing at a time.

Psychologists often describe this using two systems of thinking. System 1 is fast, automatic, and emotional. It produces quick judgements and simple shortcuts that help us move through life without analysing every decision. System 2 is slower and more deliberate. It is what we usually call "thinking."

Although we feel like System 2 is in charge, System 1 is often the real driver—shaping choices before we notice.

This becomes clear in a simple example described by Daniel Kahneman in *Thinking, Fast and Slow*:

A bat and a ball cost £1.10 in total. The bat costs £1 more than the ball. What does the ball cost?

Most people answer 10 pence. It feels right. But the correct answer is 5 pence.

System 1 produces an immediate answer. System 2 often accepts it without checking.

Part of the problem is that our brains were shaped for a very different world. Our ancestors survived by reacting quickly to danger, not by analysing probabilities. A rustle in the grass might have meant a predator. Acting fast mattered more than being precise.

That instinct still operates today. We react strongly to feelings and protect our sense of self. This is why a small insult or minor inconvenience can trigger a response that feels larger than the situation deserves.

We also have a strong need to make sense of the world, even when it is uncertain. In *The Black Swan*, Taleb describes the narrative fallacy—the tendency to create neat stories after events occur. These stories make the world feel orderly, even when it is not.

He illustrates this with an example around the capture of Saddam Hussein. At one moment, market movements were explained as evidence that the capture would not reduce terrorism. Shortly after, similar movements were explained as proof that it would improve stability. The same event supported opposite explanations within minutes. The story changed to fit the outcome.

This reflects a deeper issue. We struggle to accept that events may not have clear, immediate causes. We prefer a simple explanation over uncertainty—even if that explanation is wrong.

Understanding this creates a problem.

You can recognise these patterns.

You can explain them clearly.

And still make the same mistake in the moment.

Because most decisions are not made in calm conditions, they are made quickly, under pressure, and often with emotion already in motion. In those moments, awareness alone is not enough.

This is the gap.

The gap between knowing and doing.

Between recognising a bias and avoiding it.

Between understanding a mistake and not repeating it.

To deal with this, awareness is not enough. We need structure. This structure can be reduced to a simple loop: pause, examine, decide, and review. Each step is simple. The difficulty is remembering to use it when it matters.

A set of simple rules that can operate when thinking is fast, incomplete, and under pressure.

In other words, heuristics.

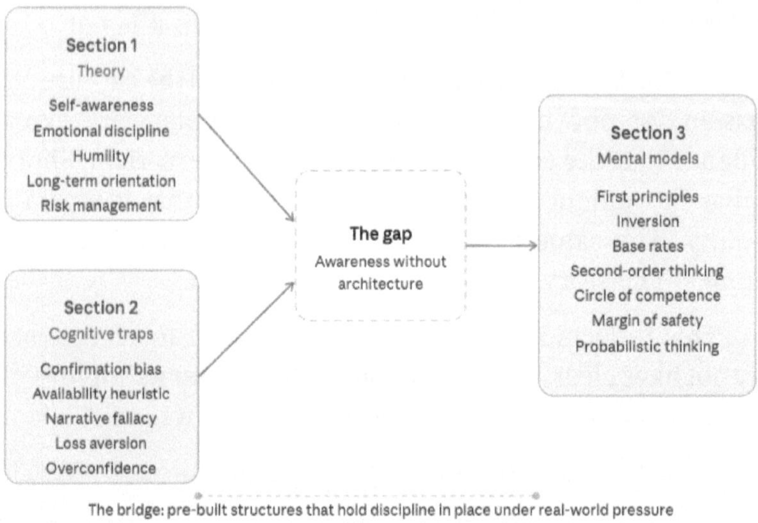

Heuristics: Fast but Flawed

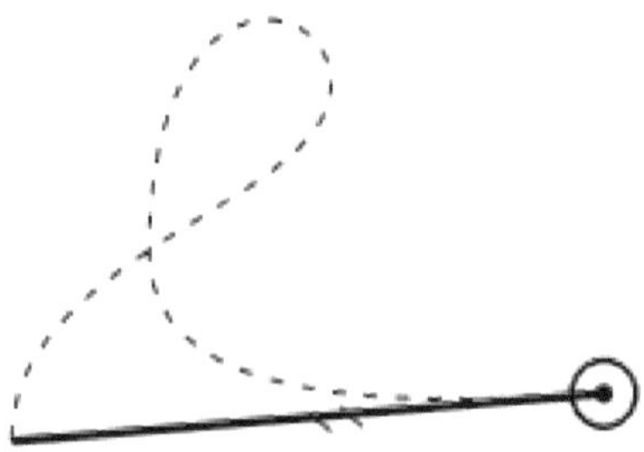

The shortcut that helps you decide can also lead you astray.

Heuristics are the mind's way of coping with a world that throws too much at us. They allow us to make decisions quickly, often with limited effort. That is not a weakness. It is necessary.

But these shortcuts are not built for accuracy in every situation. Because they favour speed over precision, they can quietly lead us into predictable mistakes.

One of the clearest warning signs is when a hard question is replaced by an easier one without us noticing. You might ask whether a stock is a good investment, but end up answering whether you like the company's products. The ease of the answer feels reassuring. Yet if a judgement comes instantly and with strong confidence, it is often a sign that the real question has been sidestepped.

A similar signal appears when thinking feels smooth and effortless. Psychologists call this cognitive ease. It is a comfortable state, but it often means we are not thinking deeply. In this state, we are more likely to accept claims, feel overconfident, and miss flaws in reasoning. When there is no sense of mental strain, the more careful part of the mind is usually inactive.

Our mental energy also plays a role. When we are tired, distracted, or under pressure, we rely more heavily on shortcuts. Decisions made late in the day or under urgency tend to favour what feels easiest rather than what is most accurate. Stress amplifies this effect, making us more susceptible to quick judgements, social influence, and artificial urgency.

Another trap lies in how we use information. The mind tends to assume that what it sees is all there is. It builds a coherent story from the available data and ignores what may be missing. If everything seems to fit too well, it is often worth asking what has been left out. Reality is rarely as clean as the stories we construct.

There is also the risk of relying too heavily on a single way of thinking. When we use the same model for every problem, we begin to force situations to fit it. As Charlie Munger often points out, a person with only a hammer sees every problem as a nail. Good judgement requires multiple perspectives that can challenge each other.

Patterns from the past can mislead us as well. When something has worked repeatedly, we begin to expect it will continue. This is sometimes described as the "turkey problem"—a long period of stability followed by a sudden and unexpected shock. At the same time, we construct explanations that make outcomes feel predictable, even when chance plays a large role.

Our bodies sometimes recognise problems before our conscious mind does. A feeling of unease or tension can signal that something does not align. Paying attention to these signals can create a pause, giving us time to think more clearly.

Finally, experience itself can become a trap. As behaviours become automatic, we stop examining them. Familiar routines feel safe, so we repeat them without question. Over time, this can lead to a kind of mental drift, where habits continue even when they no longer serve us well.

Heuristics are not the enemy. They are essential tools.

But they work best when we recognise their limits.

THE SHIFT

The goal is not to eliminate fast thinking. That is neither possible nor desirable.

The goal is to train it.

Heuristics, when left unexamined, become biases. But when understood and refined, they become tools.

They are not shortcuts. They are safeguards against predictable mistakes.

In the chapters that follow, we will move from understanding how the mind fails to building practical ways of thinking that hold up under real-world conditions.

Because, in the end, better decisions do not come from knowing more.

They come from having structures that work when it matters most.

A good heuristic applied in the wrong context becomes a bias.

MOVEMENT IV – HEURISTICS FOR BETTER JUDGEMENT

How to Use These Heuristics

The heuristics in this section are simple.

That is their strength and also their limitation.

They are not rules.

They are not a checklist to follow mechanically.

They are ways of looking at a problem from different angles.

Used well, they improve judgement.

Used blindly, they become another source of error.

DO NOT USE THEM ALL AT ONCE

It is tempting to apply every heuristic to every decision.

That usually creates confusion.

Instead:

- Use one or two that feel most relevant
- Let them clarify the situation
- Move forward with what becomes clearer

Clarity comes from focus, not from stacking tools.

USE THEM WHEN SOMETHING FEELS OBVIOUS

Heuristics are most valuable when:

- A decision feels easy
- A story feels convincing
- Confidence appears quickly

These are often the moments when thinking is weakest.

When something feels obvious, pause.

That is your signal to apply a tool.

COMBINE, DON'T ISOLATE

Each heuristic shows one part of reality.

Real insight often comes from combining them.

For example:

- First Principles → what must be true
- Inversion → what could go wrong
- Probabilistic Thinking → how likely is each outcome

Together, they create a fuller picture than anyone alone.

ALWAYS CHECK THE LIMITS

Every heuristic has blind spots. Applied in the wrong context, it becomes a bias.

- First principles can ignore practical constraints.
- Inversion can make you too cautious.
- Probabilistic thinking can create false precision.

The goal is not to trust the tool.

It is to use the tool—and then question it.

USE THEM TO IMPROVE PROCESS, NOT GUARANTEE OUTCOMES

A good decision can still lead to a bad result.

A poor decision can sometimes work out.

Heuristics do not eliminate this.

They help you:

- make better decisions more consistently,
- reduce avoidable mistakes,
- improve your process over time.

LET THEM BECOME HABIT

At first, these tools will feel deliberate.

You will have to:

- stop
- think
- apply them consciously

Over time, they should become automatic.

Not as rigid rules, but as quiet checks in the background.

A FINAL REMINDER

These heuristics are not here to make you certain.

They are here to make you **less certain for the right reasons.**

Use them not to be right,

but to avoid being wrong in predictable ways.

First Principles

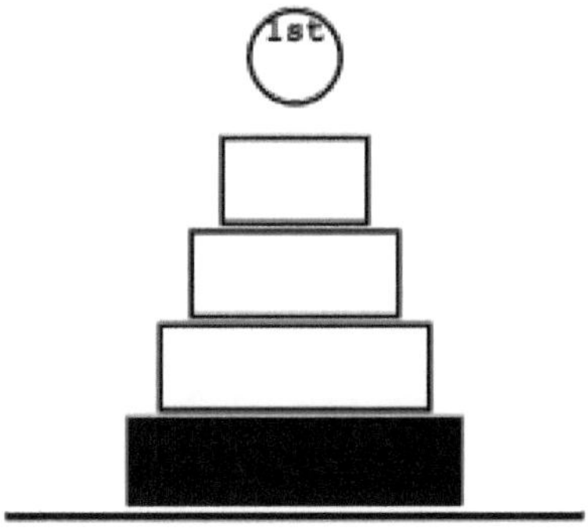

FIRST PRINCIPLES

build from the foundation

Don't ask what others do—ask what must be true.

THE HEURISTIC

Most of us move through life by copying what we see around us. We pick careers, buy things, and form opinions because they seem to work for other people. This habit is called reasoning by analogy. It saves time and effort. It works well for small decisions, but it often breaks down when the stakes are high.

There is another way to think, and it asks more of us. It is called first principles thinking. Instead of copying what already exists, you break a problem down to what is undeniably true. You strip away habits, assumptions, and what people call 'common sense'. Then you build your answer from the ground up. It is slower, but it gives you a clearer view of what is actually possible.

A clear picture of this approach appears in *Elon Musk* by Walter Isaacson. Musk treats most rules as suggestions and respects only the laws of physics as fixed. He ignores what others have done and asks what must be true.

You can see this in how he approached rockets. At the time, rockets were considered prohibitively expensive, and private companies stayed away. Most people accepted those prices because they had always been that way. Musk asked a simpler question: what are rockets made of?

He found that the raw materials—aluminium, titanium, copper, and carbon fibre—were surprisingly cheap. In some cases, they made up only a small fraction of the final price. He compared the cost of materials to the price of the finished rocket and found a large gap. He called this the 'idiot index'. If something costs far more than its parts, then the process, not the physics, is likely the problem.

One example stands out. A component called a half-nozzle jacket was priced at 13,000 dollars, yet contained only about 200 dollars' worth of steel. By returning to the basics, Musk realised the same function could be achieved far more cheaply. He did not accept industry pricing as the truth. He followed the constraints of materials.

This pattern appears again in satellite design. Engineers rebuilt systems from scratch, repeatedly asking "why" until complex assemblies became simpler ones. In some cases, multiple components were combined into one. The result was lower cost and higher efficiency—not through incremental improvement, but through reduction.

The same mindset shaped Tesla's approach to self-driving. While many engineers believed systems required radar and LiDAR, Musk argued from a different starting point. Humans drive using vision. If that is sufficient for biological systems, then a machine should be able to do the same with cameras and software. Whether one agrees or not, the reasoning begins from fundamentals rather than convention.

There is a simple structure behind this way of thinking:

- **Axioms**: identify what must be true
- **Deconstruction**: break the problem into basic parts
- **Reconstruction**: build a new solution from those parts

In *The Almanack of Naval Ravikant*, Naval explains that knowledge forms a chain. You cannot understand advanced ideas without understanding the basics beneath them. First principles thinking forces you to return to that base.

This approach also applies inward. Many of our habits and beliefs were formed early in life. Over time, they feel fixed. We stop questioning them. First principles thinking asks whether those beliefs are still valid. Instead of accepting them as identity, we test whether they are true and useful.

In *Atomic Habits*, James Clear describes how identity is shaped through repeated action. Each small behaviour reinforces who we believe we are. First principles thinking allows us to revisit those identities and rebuild them consciously.

The danger of relying only on analogy is captured in a story from *Antifragile*. A turkey is fed every day and becomes more confident that the system is safe. Then, just before Thanksgiving, that pattern breaks. The past gave the turkey confidence, but it did not reveal the truth. Patterns can mislead when we do not understand what drives them.

In *Thinking, Fast and Slow*, Daniel Kahneman describes the effort required for this kind of thinking as System 2. It is slow, deliberate, and energy-intensive. Most of the time, we rely on faster thinking because it is easier. First principles thinking pushes us to slow down and examine assumptions more carefully.

It is not a magic tool. Ignoring convention can lead to insight, but it can also lead to mistakes. Some rules exist because they reflect hard-earned lessons. Without understanding those lessons, rejecting them can backfire.

There is also the question of skill. You cannot reason from first principles without understanding the basics. Without that foundation, breaking things apart can become guesswork.

In *Clear Thinking*, Shane Parrish makes a grounded point. Success often comes from being consistently not stupid rather than brilliantly clever. People who do well tend to understand fundamentals and avoid simple mistakes.

In practice, this heuristic becomes useful at specific moments. When something feels too expensive, too complex, or simply 'the way things are done', that is often the signal to pause.

Instead of asking what others are doing, ask what must be true.

First principles thinking begins when you replace imitation with understanding.

IN PRACTICE

Thinking from first principles means reducing a problem until only the basic truths remain. What is left should be simple, even if the situation itself is complex. A useful warning, often associated with Richard Feynman, is that knowledge built through imitation

First principles thinking, at its core, is a way of seeing through complexity without getting lost in it.

LIMITS AND BLIND SPOTS

The clarity of first principles thinking makes it powerful. But that same clarity can create overconfidence.

It is easy to believe you are reasoning from fundamentals when you are simply replacing one assumption with another. If the underlying knowledge is weak, what looks like first principles may just be intuition dressed as logic.

There is also a tendency to dismiss existing practices too quickly. It can feel intelligent to ignore convention and start from scratch. Yet many rules exist because someone learned through failure. Not every constraint is arbitrary, and not every system is inefficient.

Another risk is cognitive illusion. As Daniel Kahneman explains, the mind prefers simple, coherent explanations. Even when we believe we are thinking carefully, fast intuition can still guide us. Under pressure, this becomes more likely.

Skill matters. First principles thinking depends on a strong understanding of fundamentals. Without that base, breaking problems apart leads to guesswork rather than insight.

As Shane Parrish notes in *Clear Thinking*, success often comes from avoiding simple mistakes rather than chasing clever ideas. This is especially true here. First principles thinking is not about being different. It is about being correct at the most basic level.

In the end, it is a powerful tool but not a licence to ignore reality.

It works best when paired with humility, patience and a willingness to question your own conclusions.

The goal is not just to break things down, but to rebuild them on solid ground.

Inversion

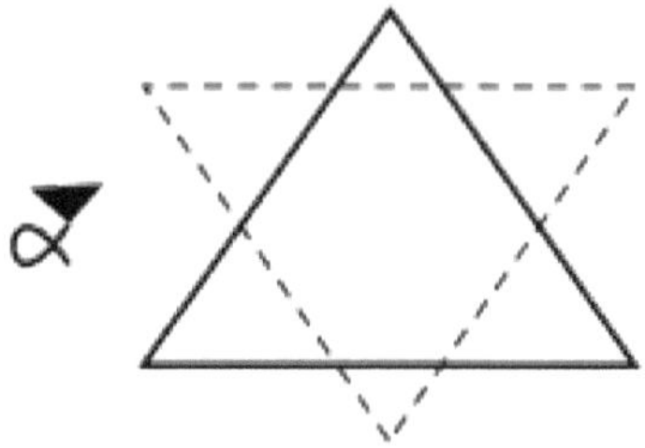

INVERSION

think it backwards

Avoiding stupidity is often more powerful than seeking brilliance.

THE HEURISTIC

Inversion is a way of thinking by starting at the end and working backwards. Instead of only asking what you want to achieve, you also ask what you want to avoid.

This simple shift often makes problems easier to understand.

It is closely linked to the idea of *via negativa*—improving things by removing what does not work rather than adding more. In complex situations, this approach is often more reliable. It is easier to identify what is clearly wrong than to define what is perfectly right.

The mathematician Carl Jacobi captured this idea in a simple phrase:

"Invert, always invert."

Hard problems often become clearer when viewed in reverse.

This way of thinking is central to the approach of Charlie Munger. As discussed in *Charlie Munger: The Complete Investor*, Munger focuses less on brilliance and more on avoiding error. His view is that it is often easier to avoid being consistently wrong than to try to be exceptionally right.

He expresses this plainly:

Success often comes from being 'consistently not stupid'.

In *Poor Charlie's Almanack*, Munger shares a simple story. A man says he wishes he knew where he would die, so he would never go there. The idea sounds naïve, but the logic is powerful. If you understand what leads to failure, you can avoid it.

A similar mindset appears in *Antifragile*, where Taleb explains *via negativa*. Removing harm is often more effective than adding benefits. Avoiding damage tends to be more reliable than trying to optimise outcomes.

Taleb also highlights a deeper truth about knowledge. It is often easier to disprove than to prove. One counterexample can break a theory, while no number of confirming cases can fully establish it. This asymmetry makes elimination a powerful tool.

The same idea appears in practical decision-making. In *The Almanack of Naval Ravikant*, Naval Ravikant explains that he focuses less on predicting what will work and more on eliminating what clearly will not. Avoiding bad decisions is often more reliable than chasing perfect ones.

In engineering, this thinking becomes tangible. Teams often add complexity without questioning whether something should exist at all. A better approach is to remove unnecessary parts first. If nothing important needs to be added back, then the system was overbuilt to begin with.

This subtractive logic applies across domains:

- In health, removing harmful habits often matters more than adding new interventions
- In behaviour, eliminating triggers is more effective than relying on willpower
- In investing, rejecting poor opportunities matters more than finding perfect ones

In practice, inversion becomes useful at specific moments:

- When a situation feels uncertain → ask what could go wrong
- When something looks attractive → ask what must go right
- When a decision feels urgent → ask what happens if you do nothing

Instead of asking, *"How do I succeed?"*, ask:

"How do I fail?"

Then avoid those paths.

That shift—from optimisation to elimination—is where inversion begins.

IN PRACTICE

In investing, inversion begins with a simple but uncomfortable question:

How is money most often lost?

This reframes the problem. Instead of chasing returns, the focus shifts to avoiding permanent loss.

This approach is central to the thinking of Pulak Prasad in *What I Learned About Investing from Darwin*. His framework emphasises rejection over selection. The key skill is not identifying great businesses, but filtering out those that can damage capital.

The logic is straightforward.

If big mistakes are avoided, compounding can take care of the rest.

This leads to a focus on reducing **Type I errors**—investing in bad businesses—rather than worrying about **Type II errors**, which are missing good ones. In practice, this means being comfortable sitting out many opportunities.

Periods of market excitement make this especially relevant.

Around 2021, the Indian speciality chemicals and amines space saw strong interest. Narratives around global supply chain shifts and "China-plus-one" themes drove enthusiasm. Many companies were newly listed, and the stories were compelling.

An inversion approach asks a different question.

Not: *What could go right?*

But: *What could go wrong?*

In many of these cases:

- Demand was cyclical.
- Margins were volatile.
- Business models were hard to evaluate.

- Valuations assumed strong execution.

When the downside depends on multiple uncertain factors, the decision becomes simpler. You step aside.

A similar pattern appears in companies like Sun Pharma Advanced Research Company (SPARC). The investment case often depends on future pipeline success rather than current cash generation.

An inversion lens does not need to predict whether the pipeline will succeed. It asks whether the current structure—negative cash flow, uncertainty, and dependence on approvals—fits within a "do not lose money" framework.

If the answer is unclear, avoidance becomes a rational decision.

This is how rejection works in practice.

Pulak Prasad formalises this through filters. His rejection list includes:

- Weak governance
- High debt
- Unclear business models
- Serial acquisitions
- Fast-changing industries
- Misaligned incentives

The goal is not to refine marginal decisions. It is to eliminate entire categories of risk early.

This approach mirrors survival logic in nature. A deer does not optimise for the best food. It prioritises avoiding predators. Missing a meal is survivable. Being wrong about safety is not.

The same applies to capital.

Missing opportunities is acceptable.

Permanent loss is not.

This connects directly to the ideas in *Antifragile*. Systems should be built to survive shocks, not to predict them. In investing, this means avoiding fragility—high leverage, opaque accounting, or dependence on fragile narratives.

Valuation provides another lens.

When a business requires:

- Sustained high growth
- Stable margins
- Flawless execution

Then multiple conditions must hold for the investment to work. This creates fragility. Inversion reframes the question:

What happens if even one assumption fails?

If the answer is a severe downside, the structure is weak.

Inversion also applies to behaviour.

Many poor outcomes come not from poor selection, but from excessive activity. Investors feel pressure to act, especially in rising markets. Prasad's idea of "being very lazy" challenges this. If good businesses compound over time, unnecessary action becomes a source of risk.

In this sense, doing nothing can be a decision.

This aligns with ideas from *The Intelligent Investor*, where Ben Graham describes how investor behaviour often causes more damage than market conditions. Avoiding interference can be as important as making good choices.

When these ideas are combined, a pattern emerges.

Inversion does not require predicting failure.

It requires recognising structures that historically lead to it.

Once those patterns are clear, the simplest move is often to exclude them.

In the end, inversion in investing is not pessimism.

It is protection.

LIMITS AND BLIND SPOTS

Inversion is appealing because it feels simple and grounded. It focuses on avoiding obvious mistakes rather than chasing perfect answers. That clarity can be powerful, but it can also create a false sense of safety.

Avoiding errors is not the same as understanding the full picture.

A useful reminder comes from Charlie Munger. While he emphasises avoiding stupidity, this idea can be misapplied. If you only focus on what can go wrong, you may become too cautious and miss opportunities that are worth taking.

Avoiding mistakes is important.

But avoiding action altogether can be a mistake of its own.

There is also the risk of incomplete elimination. As Nassim Taleb explains, removing visible risks is useful only if you understand what truly causes harm. Hidden fragility can remain even when surface risks are removed.

Another subtle trap is overconfidence.

Inversion can make decisions feel clean and decisive. You reject an idea, and the clarity feels reassuring. But as Kahneman explains in *Thinking, Fast and Slow*, the mind prefers simple, coherent narratives. Even cautious thinking can be influenced by hidden assumptions.

There is also a balance to maintain.

Inversion works best as a filter, not as a complete decision system. If every decision becomes an exercise in rejection, your perspective can become too narrow. Good judgement still requires engagement with complexity, not just avoidance of it.

In the end, inversion is a tool for protection, not a guarantee of success.

It helps reduce avoidable errors, but it does not remove uncertainty.

Used well, it creates discipline.

Used blindly, it can lead to excessive caution or misplaced confidence.

The goal is not just to avoid being wrong, but to remain aware of what you may still be missing.

Probabilistic Thinking

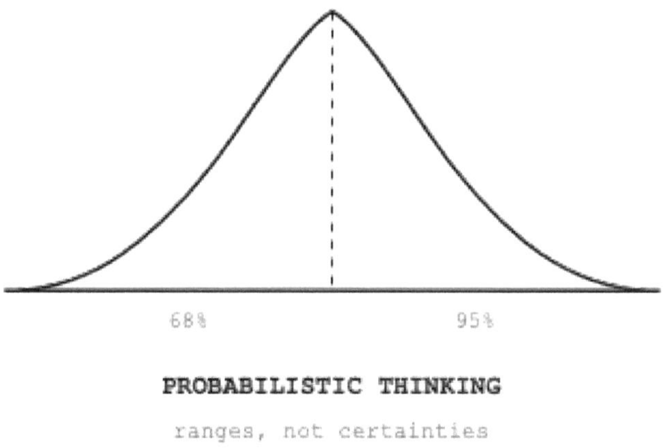

Don't ask what will happen—ask what is likely.

THE HEURISTIC

Most people think about the future as if it were a single path waiting to be discovered.

Clear thinkers see something else.

They see a range of possible outcomes, each with a different likelihood. This is probabilistic thinking. It replaces certainty with estimation and asks not *what will happen*, but *what is likely to happen—and how much it matters.*

This shift is essential because the future is not fixed. It is shaped by uncertainty, chance and incomplete information.

The human mind, however, is not naturally built for this.

As Kahneman explains in *Thinking, Fast and Slow*, our thinking operates through two systems. System 1 is fast, intuitive, and emotional. It evolved for survival, where quick reactions mattered more than accuracy. System 2 is slower and more analytical. It is capable of reasoning about probabilities, but it requires effort.

Most of the time, System 1 dominates.

That creates a problem.

Instead of thinking in probabilities, we prefer simple, coherent stories. In *The Black Swan*, Nassim Taleb calls this the *narrative fallacy*. We turn the past into neat explanations and assume the future will behave the same way.

But reality is often discontinuous.

Taleb's famous example of the turkey makes this clear. A turkey is fed every day and becomes increasingly confident that life is safe. Each observation reinforces that belief. Then, without warning, it is slaughtered. What looked like stability was only a limited view of reality.

The lesson is not about prediction. It is about perspective.

Probabilistic thinking shifts attention from stories to distributions.

Instead of asking:

- *Will this work?*

You ask:

- *What are the possible outcomes?*
- *How likely is each one?*
- *What happens if I am wrong?*

This leads naturally to the idea of **expected value**—weighing outcomes by both their size and their probability. As discussed in *Behavioural Investing* by James Montier, people often focus on how often they are right rather than how much they gain or lose.

But frequency is not what matters.

A strategy that wins often but loses heavily can still fail. A strategy that wins rarely but gains significantly can still succeed.

This is why process matters more than outcome.

Montier illustrates this through a story retold by Paul DePodesta. A blackjack player hits on 17—a statistically poor decision—and wins. The dealer says, "Nice hit." The outcome looks correct, but the decision was still wrong.

Over time, bad processes lose.

Good processes, even with bad short-term results, tend to win.

Another key distinction is between **risk** and **uncertainty**.

- Risk: probabilities are known or can be estimated (like a casino game)
- Uncertainty: probabilities themselves are unclear (like starting a business or investing in emerging sectors)

The mistake—what Taleb calls the *ludic fallacy*—is treating real life like a game with fixed odds.

In reality, many systems have **fat tails**, where extreme outcomes occur more often than expected. These events dominate results but are difficult to predict.

Because of this, probabilistic thinking requires humility.

It also requires precision.

Research from *Superforecasting* by Philip Tetlock shows that vague terms like "likely" mean very different things to different people. Assigning numbers forces clarity and allows feedback. Over time, this improves calibration—how well your expectations match reality.

Finally, because uncertainty cannot be eliminated, it must be managed.

This is where the **margin of safety**, introduced by Ben Graham, becomes essential. You build room for error, not because you expect to be wrong, but because you know you might be.

In the end, probabilistic thinking is not about prediction.

It is about positioning.

You are not trying to be certain.

You are trying to be less wrong over time.

IN PRACTICE

Probabilistic thinking becomes most visible in environments where outcomes are uneven, uncertain and difficult to predict.

Small biotech is one such domain.

Many investors approach it as a binary problem: success or failure. A drug either works or it does not. A company either scales or collapses.

But this framing hides the real structure.

Biotech outcomes are not binary—they are distributed. There are many failures, a few successes, and rare outliers.

The difficulty lies in estimating where any single company sits within that distribution.

At first glance, the upside can appear compelling. A successful drug can generate enormous returns. But probabilistic thinking forces a different question:

How likely is that outcome?

In most early-stage biotech companies:

- Cash flows are weak or negative.
- Survival depends on funding.
- Outcomes hinge on a small number of trials.
- Probabilities are not stable or easily observable.

This is not just a risk. It is **uncertainty**.

The probabilities themselves are unclear.

This makes expected value difficult to estimate with confidence. Even if the upside is large, the probability of reaching it may be extremely low. Worse, the downside is often total loss.

This creates a skewed distribution:

- Many small or total losses
- Few large winners

In theory, such distributions can still be attractive. In practice, they require an informational edge—deep technical understanding, access to data, or specialised expertise.

Without that edge, the investor is guessing.

This is where Charlie Munger's observation becomes relevant. Without a grasp of probability, you are at a structural disadvantage. In domains like biotech, that disadvantage is amplified.

The challenge is not just analytical, but behavioural.

Success stories create powerful narratives. A company that succeeds appears obvious in hindsight. Its path is reconstructed as logical and predictable. Failures disappear into the background.

This distorts perception.

As Daniel Kahneman describes, coherence is often mistaken for likelihood. A story that makes sense feels probable, even when it is not.

This is why probabilistic thinking often leads not to action, but to restraint.

Avoiding small biotech is not a rejection of uncertainty. It is a selection of which uncertainty to engage with.

Instead of asking:

- *Can this succeed?*

You ask:

- *Can I estimate the odds with any confidence?*

If the answer is no, stepping aside becomes a rational decision.

This is reinforced by the idea of **margin of safety**. In small biotech, the downside is often irreversible. A failed trial or funding gap can destroy value quickly. There is little buffer for error.

Even position sizing does not fully solve the problem. Binary outcomes can dominate results regardless of allocation size.

From a probabilistic perspective, the decision becomes clearer.

You are not avoiding upside.

You are avoiding **opaque probability distributions**.

Instead, capital is directed toward areas where:

- Probabilities are more stable
- Outcomes are more continuous
- Information is more accessible

This does not eliminate uncertainty.

It makes it more manageable.

In this sense, probabilistic thinking operates at two levels:

1. Evaluating individual opportunities
2. Choosing which domains are worth evaluating at all

The second is often more important than the first.

LIMITS AND BLIND SPOTS

Probabilistic thinking brings realism and discipline. It replaces certainty with estimation and encourages better decisions under uncertainty.

But it has its own limits.

A key risk is the **illusion of precision.**

As Taleb argues in *The Black Swan*, rare and extreme events often sit outside our models. These events dominate outcomes but are difficult to anticipate. Probability estimates can therefore appear accurate while missing what matters most.

You can be precise—and still be wrong.

Another danger is that probabilities can become **dressed-up narratives.**

As Daniel Kahneman explains, the mind prefers coherent stories. When a scenario feels logical, we assign it a higher probability, even if the evidence is weak. Numbers can then give a false sense of objectivity.

Expected value has a similar limitation.

While mathematically sound, it depends on inputs that are often uncertain. If both outcomes and probabilities are poorly understood, expected value becomes fragile. The calculation is only as good as its assumptions.

There is also a behavioural trade-off.

Thinking in probabilities can slow decision-making. When every outcome is uncertain, it becomes tempting to keep refining estimates and waiting for clarity. This can lead to analysis paralysis, where the fear of being wrong prevents action.

In such cases, the tool meant to improve judgement becomes a source of delay.

Finally, probabilistic thinking can encourage excessive caution.

If every decision is framed in terms of downside risk, you may avoid situations that are uncertain but worthwhile. Not all uncertainty is harmful. Some of it is necessary for growth.

In the end, probabilistic thinking is a tool for humility, not control.

It helps you navigate uncertainty, but it does not remove it.

Used well, it sharpens judgement.

Used blindly, it can create false precision or hesitation.

The goal is not to assign numbers to everything.

It is important to recognise where your understanding is strong, where it is weak, and where it is simply not enough.

SECOND-ORDER THINKING

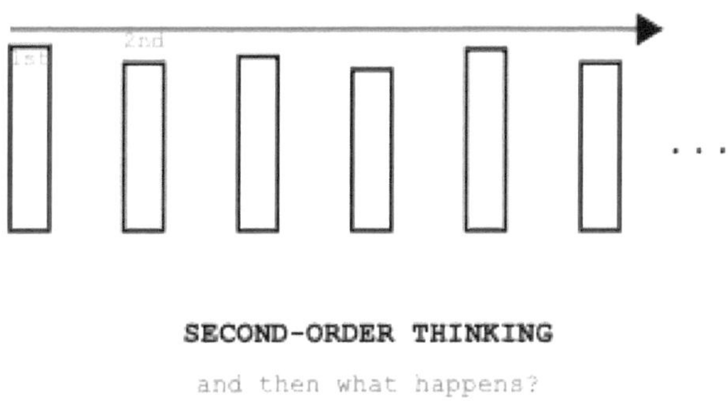

The first consequence is obvious—the second is where the edge is.

Kahneman's work on the planning fallacy shows that we focus too much on our own plan and not enough on how similar situations have actually played out.

Second-order thinking asks:

- *What usually happens in cases like this?*
- *What is different this time?*

Several tools strengthen this approach:

- **Inversion** (Charlie Munger): Ask how things fail, not just how they succeed
- **Premortem** (Gary Klein): Imagine failure in advance and work backwards
- **Opportunity cost** (Howard Marks): Every decision excludes alternatives

Each of these extends thinking beyond the immediate.

In the end, second-order thinking is not about being clever.

It is about seeing **interactions, consequences, and expectations** more clearly than the crowd.

IN PRACTICE

Second-order thinking becomes most valuable in environments where:

- Outcomes are uncertain
- Narratives are strong
- Consensus builds quickly

Markets are one such environment.

Consider a widely accepted growth theme.

The first-order view is simple:

"This trend is strong → companies in this space will do well."

Second-order thinking asks:

- What does the market already expect?
- How much optimism is already embedded in prices?
- What happens if reality is slightly worse than expectations?

This shift—from *fundamentals* to *expectations*—is critical.

As Howard Marks emphasises, the difference between a good company and a good investment lies in expectations.

A practical decision rule emerges:

"What is already priced in?"

If expectations are modest, even average outcomes can lead to gains. If expectations are extreme, even strong outcomes can disappoint.

This is why risk often feels lowest when it is actually highest.

When something appears obvious, disagreement disappears.

When disagreement disappears, protection disappears.

Second-order thinking also works through **chains of consequences**.

Take any decision and extend it:

- Strong growth → attracts competition
- More competition → reduces margins
- Lower margins → affects valuation

The first step looks attractive.

The chain may not be.

Inversion strengthens this further.

Instead of asking:

"How does this succeed?"

You ask:

"How does this fail—even if things go right?"

For example:

- A company performs well
- But valuation was too high
- Or margins compress
- Or regulation shifts

Success at the business level does not guarantee success at the investment level.

A **premortem** makes this practical.

Imagine the decision has already failed.

Then ask:

- What went wrong?
- What did I miss?
- What assumption failed?

This surfaces risks that optimism tends to hide.

Second-order thinking also requires awareness of **consensus positioning**.

If everyone believes the same thing:

- Capital flows in the same direction
- Expectations rise together
- Fragility increases

A small negative surprise can then have an outsized impact.

This is not about predicting disaster.

It is about recognising **crowded assumptions**.

Finally, second-order thinking forces you to confront **opportunity costs**.

Every decision implies:

"At the expense of what?"

Capital, time, and attention are finite.

Choosing one path quietly excludes others.

This question often reveals more than the original decision itself.

When combined, these habits form a repeatable process:

- Extend consequences
- Examine expectations
- Test failure modes
- Question consensus
- Evaluate trade-offs

The goal is not perfect prediction.

There are fewer surprises.

LIMITS AND BLIND SPOTS

Second-order thinking feels like an advantage.

It goes beyond the obvious.

It creates distance from the crowd.

But that advantage can become a trap.

The first risk is **false depth**.

As Daniel Kahneman shows, the mind can build convincing chains of reasoning from weak assumptions.

You may ask, "And then what?"—but still be guided by intuition rather than evidence.

A longer explanation is not always a better one.

The second risk is **overcomplication**.

Not every situation requires multiple layers of analysis.

As Howard Marks reminds us, success does not come from sounding sophisticated.

It comes from being right.

If your thinking becomes too abstract, you may lose sight of basic facts.

The third risk is **reflexive contrarianism**.

Second-order thinking often leads you away from the crowd.

But being different is not the goal.

Rejecting an idea simply because it is popular is just another form of bias.

As Charlie Munger emphasised:

Avoiding stupidity matters more than appearing smart.

There is also the problem of **incomplete chains**.

You can extend consequences one or two steps, but real systems are far more complex.

Beyond a point, reasoning turns into speculation.

The confidence remains.

The accuracy does not.

Finally, second-order thinking can create **decision friction**.

When every action leads to multiple possible consequences, hesitation increases.

You keep extending the chain.

You wait for clarity that never fully arrives.

This can lead to inaction.

In the end, second-order thinking is a tool for clarity—not superiority.

It helps you:

- Slow down

- See beyond the obvious
- Recognise hidden effects

But it works best when grounded in reality.

The goal is not to outthink everyone else.

It is to avoid simple mistakes while staying close to what is true.

The Map is Not the Territory

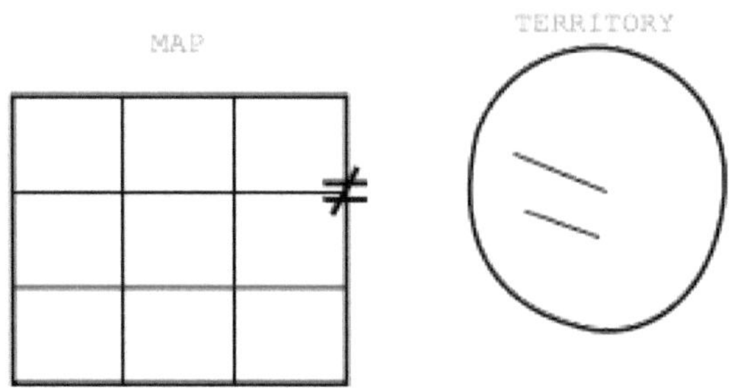

THE MAP IS NOT THE TERRITORY

the model is not the real thing

The model is useful—but it is never reality.

THE HEURISTIC

In 1931, Alfred Korzybski introduced a simple but powerful idea:

The map is not the territory.

A description of something is not the thing itself.

A model is not reality.

A menu is not the meal.

A *map* is any simplified representation of the world.

It could be:

- a financial model
- a company narrative
- a management framework
- or even a personal belief

We rely on these maps because reality is too complex to process in full. They help us act without being overwhelmed.

But they come with a cost.

Every map leaves something out.

Shane Parrish, in *The Great Mental Models: Volume 1*, illustrates this with a story from Lewis Carroll. A character proposes building a map at a scale of one mile to one mile—it would be perfectly accurate, but completely useless.

A useful map must simplify.

The problem begins when we forget that it is a simplification.

We see this clearly in everyday tools.

The London Underground map is designed for navigation, not accuracy. It distorts distance and direction to make routes easier to follow.

For passengers, it is highly useful.

For engineers or train drivers, it is not.

The same map can be right for one purpose and wrong for another.

This is the core insight:

All models are selective. None is complete.

As George Box famously said,

“All models are wrong, but some are useful.”

The key is knowing **how far a model can take you before it breaks down**.

History offers clear examples.

For centuries, Isaac Newton’s laws provided an accurate map of motion. They worked well—until conditions changed.

In 1905, Albert Einstein introduced relativity, revealing limits in Newton’s framework.

Newton’s map was not wrong.

It was incomplete.

The same pattern appears in social systems.

The idea of the **Tragedy of the Commons**, introduced by Garrett Hardin, suggests that shared resources will be overused.

But Elinor Ostrom showed that real communities often manage shared resources effectively.

The model described one outcome.

Reality contained many.

Maps are also shaped by perspective.

They reflect:

- What is measured
- What is ignored
- What the creator values

This makes them powerful—but also biased.

As historian Margaret MacMillan notes, many national borders reflect political decisions rather than cultural realities. They are maps imposed on territory.

There is a greater danger.

Maps do not just describe reality.

They can begin to **shape it**.

Frederick Winslow Taylor's scientific management model improved efficiency—but also treated people as machines. Over time, the model influenced behaviour itself.

When a map becomes rigid, it stops guiding and starts distorting.

To use maps well, a few principles help:

- Treat reality as the final test
- Update models when evidence changes
- Ask what the map leaves out
- Understand who created it and why

In the end, maps are essential.

But they are always partial, always simplified, and always slightly out of date.

They are guides—not truth.

IN PRACTICE

The idea that the map is not the territory becomes most useful in situations where reality is complex, but the metrics are simple. Business analysis is one such setting.

Consider how investors often judge companies.

The map is straightforward:

"More clients or more projects → stronger business → higher earnings power."

Now apply this to Syngene International.

It reports around 400 innovators or customers.

At first glance, this suggests scale, diversification, and resilience.

Place it beside Sai Life Sciences.

It has fewer visible projects.

The map leads to a quick conclusion about relative strength.

BUT THE TERRITORY TELLS A DIFFERENT STORY.

Most of Syngene's work sits in early-stage drug discovery.

This is a fail-fast environment:

- Many projects do not progress
- Revenues per project are small
- Outcomes are uncertain

Sai operates differently:

- Greater focus on late-stage and commercial manufacturing
- Deeper client relationships, including commercial manufacturing for big pharma
- Higher value per programme

The shift is subtle but critical.

It is not the number of projects that matters.

It is the value created by each one.

Extend this further.

Companies like Divi's Labs and Laurus Labs illustrate how skewed outcomes can be.

The first-order view:

"More projects → more revenue."

The territory:

- A single blockbuster molecule can be worth ₹1000 crore
- One commercial shipment can match or exceed annual output elsewhere

The map counts activity.

The territory rewards success.

A practical decision rule emerges:

"What does this metric actually capture—and what does it hide?"

If a metric captures surface activity, it may miss economic depth.

If it captures outcomes, it may better reflect reality.

This is why simple comparisons often fail.

They compress a multi-dimensional business into a single number.

The convenience is high.

The accuracy is not.

A useful analogy helps.

Imagine judging a hotel or a hospital by the number of people entering the lobby.

The map suggests:

"More footfall → better business."

The territory asks:

- How many guests actually stay?
- How long do they stay?
- How much do they spend?

Footfall is visible.

Value is earned elsewhere.

This tension between simplification and reality was captured by Lewis Carroll in *Sylvie and Bruno*.

He describes a map so detailed that it matches the territory exactly, making it useless.

In practice, we make the opposite error.

Our maps are too simple, yet we treat them as complete.

We stop questioning what they leave out.

There is also a behavioural layer.

Once a metric becomes dominant, behaviour adapts to it.

If investors reward project counts:

- companies may optimise for volume
- pipelines may expand
- but value per project may fall

Jane Jacobs described a similar pattern in *The Death and Life of Great American Cities*.

Urban planners relied on neat models of how cities should work, then tried to force real cities to fit them.

The result was often worse outcomes, not better ones.

The lesson is not to reject maps.

It is to choose better ones.

A more useful lens in CRDMO would focus on:

- Value per relationship
- Share of revenue from commercial manufacturing
- Durability of each programme

These are harder to measure.

But they are closer to reality.

The same principle applies to financial ratios.

Pulak Prasad, in *What I Learned About Investing from Darwin*, advocates focusing on high ROCE businesses.

It is a powerful heuristic.

But like all heuristics, it is still a map.

Consider Neuland Labs.

The map (in 2019) said:

"ROCE is 4% → weak business."

The territory was evolving:

- Capabilities were improving
- Commercial opportunities were building
- Future returns were changing

By the time reported ROCE reached 30%, the stock had already become a 50-bagger.

The map improved only after the territory had already shifted.

This leads to a deeper distinction:

- Reported ROCE reflects the past.
- Intrinsic ROCE reflects future earning power.

The first is visible and comfortable.

The second requires judgement, patience, and a willingness to look beyond the numbers.

As George Box observed, all models are wrong, but some are useful.

The danger lies not in using models, but in trusting them too much.

A useful checklist emerges:

- What is this metric simplifying?
- What is it leaving out?
- Is it measuring activity or value?
- Has the territory already changed?

The goal is not to discard maps.

It is to stay anchored to reality while using them.

In the end, investing rewards those who can see the gap between the map and the territory before it becomes obvious.

That gap is where mispricing lives.

A simple question to leave with.

When you look at a business, are you relying on reported ROCE, or are you trying to estimate its intrinsic ROCE before it becomes obvious to everyone else?

LIMITS AND BLIND SPOTS

The idea that the map is not the territory feels intuitive.

It encourages deeper thinking and scepticism towards simple metrics.

But this advantage can create its own problems.

The first risk is overcorrection.

In trying to avoid simple metrics, you may dismiss useful signals.

Not every simple measure is misleading.

Sometimes, a high-level metric captures enough truth to be decision-worthy.

The second risk is false insight.

It is easy to believe you are seeing the "real" territory when you are simply replacing one map with another.

The distinction feels sophisticated, but it may still rest on assumptions that are hard to verify.

Confidence can rise faster than accuracy.

The third risk is narrative bias.

When you move away from numbers, you often rely more on stories about the future.

These stories can be compelling but fragile.

Without discipline, they can drift away from evidence.

There is also the challenge of timing.

Even if your view of intrinsic value is correct, markets may take time to recognise it.

The gap between map and territory can persist longer than expected.

This creates pressure on both conviction and patience.

Finally, there is the risk of complexity.

Reality is messy, but not every decision requires deep reconstruction.

If every metric is questioned and every assumption unpacked, decision-making can slow down.

Clarity can give way to paralysis.

In the end, the goal is not to reject maps or to outthink them entirely. It is to use them with awareness.

Good judgement lies in knowing when a map is sufficient, and when it is hiding something important.

Silent Evidence

What you don't see often matters more than what you do.

THE HEURISTIC

Success stories are everywhere.

They are easy to see, easy to remember, and easy to believe. But they often hide more than they reveal.

Nassim Taleb calls this problem **silent evidence** in *The Black Swan*. It describes what happens when we judge reality based only on what survived, while ignoring everything that failed and disappeared.

What is missing matters as much as what is visible.

A simple illustration comes from Cicero.

He was shown paintings of sailors who survived shipwrecks after praying to the gods. The message was clear: prayer brings safety.

Cicero asked a better question:

Where are the paintings of those who prayed and still drowned?

Those unseen sailors are the silent evidence.

Because they did not survive, their stories were never told. The result is a distorted view of cause and effect.

Taleb offers another example through Giacomo Casanova.

Casanova survived countless risks and came to believe he was unusually lucky, even skilled at escaping danger. He documented his experiences in detail.

But we only hear from him because he survived.

We do not see:

- those who took similar risks
- those who made similar decisions
- those who did not make it back

The narrative feels convincing because the failures are invisible.

This bias appears in subtle ways.

Taleb calls one version the **'swimmer's body illusion'.**

We see elite swimmers and assume that swimming created their physiques.

In reality, many people swim. Very few have that body.

The missing data matters:

- people with average physiques who trained just as hard
- those who never reached the elite level

What looks like a cause may actually be selection.

A similar distortion appears in science.

Imagine an experiment where animals are exposed to extreme conditions. The survivors appear stronger.

At first glance, the treatment seems effective.

But the weaker subjects are gone.

The sample has been filtered by survival.

Without the "cemetery" of failures, the conclusion is misleading.

This is the central problem:

We overlearn from winners and underlearn from losers.

We see:

- Successful founders
- Bestselling authors
- Breakthrough companies

We do not see:

- The thousands who tried the same approach
- The equally capable individuals who failed
- The role of timing, luck, and environment

As a result, success begins to look like a formula.

Taleb reinforces this with the **turkey problem**.

A turkey is fed every day. Each day confirms that life is safe.

Then, without warning, it is killed.

From the turkey's perspective, the past looked like proof.

From reality's perspective, it was incomplete data.

This leads to a critical distinction:

Absence of evidence is not evidence of absence.

Just because failure is not visible does not mean it is unlikely.

Howard Marks makes a related point in *The Most Important Thing*.

Good outcomes can hide bad processes.

A strategy can appear safe simply because it worked—not because it was robust.

To think clearly, you must consider:

- What happened
- What could have happened
- What is missing from view

IN PRACTICE

Silent evidence becomes powerful when you apply it to real decisions.

The key shift is simple:

Do not ask only why something worked. Ask what you are not seeing.

CASE 1: TESLA – SUCCESS VS SURVIVAL BIAS

Tesla is often seen as a clear story of vision and execution.

The narrative usually highlights:

- Bold thinking
- First-principles reasoning
- Long-term strategy

But this view is incomplete.

In the early 2000s, Tesla was not inevitable. It was fragile.

At the same time, several companies pursued similar ideas:

- Better Place
- Fisker Automotive
- Coda Automotive

They had:

- Funding
- Talent
- Strong narratives

They failed.

This is the silent evidence.

When you look only at Tesla, success appears logical. When you include the failures, the environment looks uncertain and risky.

Tesla's approach—guided by Elon Musk—did reveal real insights:

- Batteries could be cheaper at the material level.
- Manufacturing could be redesigned.
- Software could be integrated into hardware.

But these insights showed **possibility**, not certainty.

This distinction is critical:

First principles can show that something can work.

They do not show how often it will work.

Tesla also benefited from:

- Favourable timing (battery improvements, climate awareness)
- Access to capital
- Regulatory support

Remove any of these, and the outcome may have changed.

CASE 2: NARAYANA HEALTH – WHEN A MODEL LOOKS UNIVERSAL

Narayana Health is often presented as proof that healthcare can be both high quality and low cost.

The story is compelling:

- Efficient systems
- Strong outcomes
- Lower prices

It appears repeatable.

But again, silent evidence matters.

Many hospitals have attempted similar models:

- Reducing costs
- Standardising processes
- Scaling operations

Most struggled.

Narayana Health works under specific conditions:

- **High volume** → repetition improves efficiency
- **Standardisation** → reduces variation
- **Focused procedures** → allows system-like execution

These conditions are not universal.

The mistake is assuming:

A successful outcome implies a general rule.

In reality, it may reflect a narrow set of favourable conditions.

A PRACTICAL FRAMEWORK

To apply silent evidence, shift your analysis:

1. **Look for the graveyard**

   What similar attempts failed? Why?

2. **Separate possibility from probability**

   Just because something worked does not mean it is likely to work again.

3. **Identify hidden conditions**

   What had to be true for success?

   - Timing
   - Scale
   - Regulation
   - Capital

4. **Study distributions, not stories**

   One outcome tells you very little.

   A full range of outcomes tells you much more.

5. **Ask the base rate**

   How often does this type of success actually occur?

   In the end, the goal is not to dismiss success.

   It is to place it in context.

LIMITS AND BLIND SPOTS

Silent evidence is powerful, but it has its own limits.

The first risk is **excessive scepticism**.

If you focus only on failures, you may become too cautious and miss real opportunities.

Not every success is random.

Some patterns do repeat.

The second risk is **incomplete reconstruction**.

Even when you try to account for failures, you may still miss:

- Hidden variables
- Unrecorded attempts
- Structural differences

The graveyard is rarely fully visible.

The third risk is **false precision**.

You may try to quantify probabilities without enough data.

As Taleb warns, some systems are too complex for reliable estimation.

The fourth risk is **paralysis**.

If every success is questioned, decision-making can slow down.

You still need to act—just with better awareness.

Finally, there is a deeper tension:

You can never fully see the invisible.

Silent evidence reminds you of what is missing.

But it cannot reveal everything that is missing.

In the end, the goal is balance.

Use success stories as signals—but not as proof.

Look for what is hidden—but accept that some of it will remain unseen.

The key question is not:

Why did this succeed?

But:

What am I not seeing that could change my conclusion?

CLOSING

THE UNSEEN GAME

THE UNSEEN GAME

the rules nobody told you about

The real game is not what you see. It is what you miss.

Most decisions do not look like decisions when they happen.

They feel automatic.

They feel obvious.

They feel necessary.

Something happens.

You respond.

And then you move on.

That is how most mistakes are made.

THE PATTERN YOU HAVE SEEN

Throughout this book, the same pattern appears in different forms.

Overconfidence is not just believing too much.

It is failing to pause before trusting what feels right.

Anchoring is not just a number.

It is accepting a starting point without stepping back.

The crowd and recency are not just external pressures.

They are the absence of independent thought in the moment it matters.

Narratives feel complete because they remove uncertainty too early.

Loss aversion feels rational because it protects you from discomfort now, while creating larger problems later.

These are not separate problems.

They are variations of the same mistake:

Acting without noticing.

THE SAME LESSON, REVISITED

In cricket, you see how the best bowlers do not just rely on skill.

They disrupt timing.

Jasprit Bumrah delays the release just enough to break instinct.

Ravichandran Ashwin interrupts movement and forces hesitation.

Shane Warne creates a moment before the ball is even delivered—where the batsman is already reacting.

The principle is the same.

When rhythm breaks, awareness begins.

And when awareness begins, better decisions become possible.

THE PAUSE FRAMEWORK

What has been implicit throughout this book can now be made explicit.

A simple loop:

Pause → Examine → Decide → Review

This is not a technique.

It is a structure.

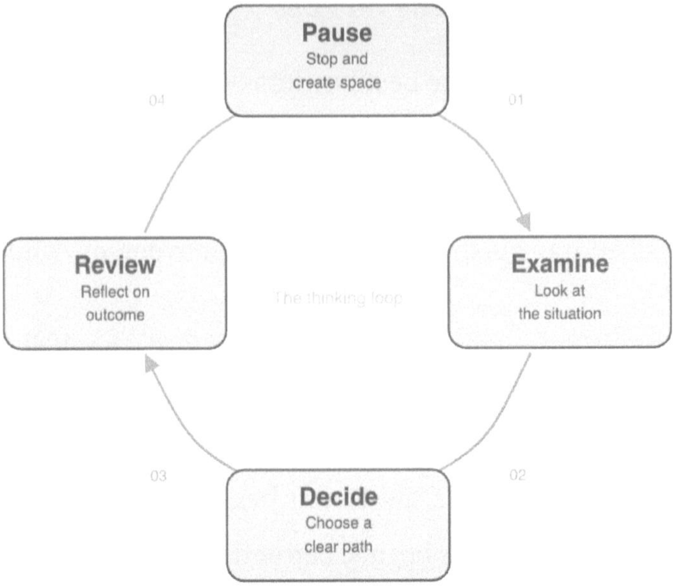

1. **Pause**

   Interrupt the automatic response.

   When something feels:

   obvious

   urgent

   certain

   that is the signal.

   The pause is not a delay for its own sake.

   It is space.

   Without it, everything that follows is reactive.

2. **Examine**

   Look at the situation clearly.

   Ask:

   What is actually happening?

What might I be missing?

What assumptions am I making?

This is where the tools in this book apply:

First principles

Inversion

Probabilistic thinking

Second-order effects

You are not trying to be perfect.

You are trying to see more than your first reaction.

3. **Decide**

   Make a choice.

   Not based on impulse.

   Not based on comfort.

   But based on the best understanding available.

   Good decisions are not certain.

   They are considered.

4. **Review**

   After the outcome, return to the decision.

   Not to judge the result—but to understand the process.

   Was the reasoning sound?

   What was missed?

   What can be improved?

   This is where learning compounds.

   Without review, mistakes repeat.

   With it, patterns become visible.

WHAT THIS CHANGES

This framework does not eliminate error.

You will still be wrong.

You will still feel pressure, uncertainty, and doubt.

But something shifts.

You begin to notice the moment before action.

You begin to recognise when thinking is weak.

You begin to separate what feels right from what is right.

And over time, that changes outcomes.

Not immediately.

Not dramatically.

But consistently.

THE UNSEEN ADVANTAGE

Most people focus on information.

Fewer focus on thinking.

Almost no one focuses on the moment between the two.

That is where the advantage lies.

Not in knowing more.

But in using what you know—at the right moment.

ONE FINAL QUESTION

The next time something feels obvious, urgent, or certain:

Will you react—

Or will you pause?

DESIGNING *THE INVESTOR'S MIND*

This book is about how we think.
It is also designed to reflect it.

Better decisions do not come from more information.
They come from better moments of thinking.

Mind is intentionally dominant.

Every decision passes through it.
Models and analysis support it—but they do not act on their own.

"Investor's" provides context.
"Mind" carries the weight.

The red dot over the "i" partially overlaps the black.

Clarity is never complete.

Even when thinking feels precise, it carries distortion—bias, blind spots, and unseen assumptions.

The black remains visible.
The red does not replace it—it interferes.

That is how thinking works.

The concentric circles represent layers of understanding.

From a distance, they appear complete.
They are not.

The partial red segments mark what cannot be fully known:

uncertainty
doubt
randomness

No process removes them.

The chapters are intentionally short.

Each one focuses on a single idea—clear enough to use, simple enough to revisit.

This is not a book to be read once.
It is a book to return to—when decisions feel obvious, urgent, or certain.

Those are the moments when thinking is weakest.

Beneath it all is a simple loop:

Pause → Examine → Decide → Review

Most mistakes happen because this loop is skipped.
Because the pause disappears.

The aim is not to slow thinking down everywhere—
only where it matters.

This book does not remove uncertainty.

It works within it.

The goal is not to be right every time.
It is to be less wrong—and to recognise when it matters.

Because in the end, the quality of your decisions depends less on what happens—

and more on what you do in the pause before you act.

Acknowledgments

I am grateful for the opportunity to think, write, and share—often through uncertainty, and often by being wrong in the short term in order to stay aligned with a longer-term purpose. This work has been shaped by real-time learning rather than hindsight, influenced in no small measure by the ideas of the late Daniel Kahneman, Nassim Nicholas Taleb, the late Charlie Munger, and others. I am thankful to my readers and subscribers who encouraged me to continue after *Framing Business Uncertainty*, and to my family and friends for their steady support throughout.

About the Author

Sajal Kapoor is an investor and thinker focused on decision-making under uncertainty.

He is the author of *Framing Business Uncertainty* and writes the widely followed Substack *Antifragile Thinking*, read by over 25,000 subscribers. On X, he shares ideas as @unseenvvalue.

His work explores how judgement breaks—and how it can be improved—across markets and life.

www.ingramcontent.com/pod-product-compliance
Ingram Content Group UK Ltd.
Pitfield, Milton Keynes, MK11 3LW, UK
UKHW040232290926
15471UKWH00002B/145

Most mistakes don't come from lack of knowledge.
They come from acting too quickly.

Something happens.
You react.

In between, there is a pause.

That moment shapes everything.

The Investor's Mind is about learning to see it—and use it.

Not by predicting better.

But by thinking clearly when it matters.

Pause → Examine → Decide → Review

You don't need more information.

You need better moments of thinking.

ISBN 979-8-90479-796-6

9 798904 797966

notionpress.com

Hussein Elasrag

The Global Financial Crisis and the Islamic Finance